Memory on My Doorstep
Chronicles of the Bataclan Neighborhood, P

Memory
on my
doorstep

Chronicles of the
Bataclan neighborhood
Paris 2015—2016

Sarah Gensburger

Leuven University Press

The book was published with the support of

The Institute for Social
sciences of Politics, UMR
7220 — CNRS — Paris
Nanterre University —
ENS Paris Saclay

The French National
Center for Scientific
Research and its
special cluster on
"Researching terrorism"

The research cluster
Labex Past in Present,
ANR-11-LABX-0026-01

This book project won a French Voices Award 2017 (Face Foundation)

The photos and chronicles which constitute the central part of this book were first published
in French in 2017 by Anamosa who authorized the reproduction of the maps designed by
Aurélie Boissière in the present case.

Translation into English: Katharine Throssell

ISBN 978 94 6270 134 2
e-ISBN 978 94 6166 279 8
D / 2019/ 1869 / 9
NUR: 756

Book Design: DOGMA

GPRC
Guaranteed
Peer Reviewed
Content
www.gprc.be

To my children, Norah and Jacob,
who have been two great research assistants here
in so many ways, and to their father Renaud,
for his constant support and love.

In Memoriam

On January 7, 2015, at noon, two terrorists broke into the offices of French satirical newspaper *Charlie Hebdo,* at 10 Rue Nicolas Appert in the 11th arrondissement of Paris. They killed eleven people. A few minutes later, as they fled the scene, they shot down a police officer named Ahmed Merabet at close range, in cold blood, outside number 62 Boulevard Richard Lenoir, two blocks away from the Bataclan concert hall.

Barely ten months later, on the night of November 13, 2015, three gunmen rushed toward the Bataclan. They began by shooting the people sitting outside the Bataclan Café at number 50 Boulevard Voltaire before going inside the concert hall itself and opening fire on the crowd. On this same night, other gunmen shot people in several other cafés and restaurants in and around the 11th arrondissement, as well as in the nearby 10th arrondissement, leaving a total of 130 people dead and almost 500 wounded.

These events all took place in the same neighborhood.

Contents

▲ November 14, 2016, Bataclan café. While taking a picture of the new tag, I accidentally realized a self-portrait.

Introduction

Between Research and Everyday Life:
Photography, Family and Ordinary Conversations

Memory studies is a flourishing field of research that is driven by trauma (Alexander, 2012). Several of the core concepts of the field are built upon the study of the memory of events labeled as "traumatic." Widespread notions such as "postmemory" (Hirsch, 2012) or "flashbulb memory" (Curci & Luminet, 2017) largely rely, for example, on the conviction that the collective memory dynamics under investigation were first generated by an original trauma. From this perspective, empirical research in the field was initially largely focused on the memory of the Holocaust, although the scope has more recently been broadened to study the memory of other genocides and mass violence. Since 2001, and particularly following 9/11, this approach has also structured several studies on the memorialization of terrorist attacks in contemporary societies.

As a result, a large portion of scholarly work in memory studies considers "traumatic memory" as ontologically distinct from everyday memory (Edkins, 2003). Using psychological concepts developed to treat individual pathologies, this approach seeks to understand the relationships between collective memory and collective trauma, and in so doing pays particular attention to the dynamics of resilience that mean societies do not collapse when they are confronted with mass crimes (Foucault, 2016). They therefore emphasize the historical rupture brought about by the event, rather than the social continuity that exists alongside it.

These studies, which are often rich and productive, and in which I participate, are often conducted using interviews with "witnesses," as was the case following the 9/11 attacks in America (Clark, Bearman, Ellis & Smith, 2011), and after the Bataclan attacks in France in 2015 (Peschanski & Eustache, 2016). They also draw on the analysis of messages written by citizens anxious to express their concern, whether these are posted on social media (Oksanen et al., 2018) or left in the streets (Truc, 2018). Terrorist attacks tend to produce an immediate memorialization,[1] in particular through grassroots memorials that develop "spontaneously" at the site of the events (Santino, 2006). The extent of the collective trauma is thus seen as explaining the mountains of messages, flowers, candles, and other objects that then occupy the public space. Conversely, and not without a certain tautology, the amount of tributes (or tweets sent and retweeted) is also seen as an indication of the level of trauma.

However, some of these studies have underlined the importance of the ordinary and everyday memory dynamics that are at the very core of remembering events considered as "traumatic." Even the flashbulb memory phenomenon itself seems best explained by taking into account everyday interactions and social factors (Talarico & Rubin, 2017; Hirst et al., 2015). Some researchers go one step further and plead for a more ordinary approach to memory dynamics, even in "traumatic contexts" and beyond the sometimes exclusive "resilience approach" (Brown & Hoskins, 2010; Heath-Kelly, 2017). In so doing, these studies do not seek to assess the intensity or the impact of traumatic experience as such, but rather to constitute a heuristic perspective on the ordinary social dynamics that may be at stake in the places and social groups where the event occurred. How can we grasp the social frameworks of memory around a "traumatic event?" How can we learn about the way people remember terrorist attacks through everyday conversations?

There are two main methodological approaches that have been used to try to answer these questions. Part of the existing literature relies on the study of social networks (Browning, 2018), on the organization of focus groups, and on conversation analysis techniques, which are unfortunately "unable to employ a pure form of conversation analysis (which normally involves recording everyday conversations without a researcher present)" (Jackson & Hall, 2016, p. 295). Other studies have dealt with the aftermath of terrorist

---

1   Immediate memorialization is not, as such, a specificity of social reactions to terrorist attacks. Recent studies have shown that the Holocaust itself gave rise to a similar dynamic (Diner, 2009; Cesarani & Sundquist, 2011), including in France (Perego, 2016; Azouvi, 2012). However, this has only very rarely taken the form of a grassroots memorial, notably because of the geographic dispersal of survivors, and their social marginalization in the post-war period.

attacks from a spatial perspective and through the lens of the neighborhoods where people live (Heath-Kelly, 2016; Tota, 2004). Once again, 9/11 is the focus of most of the studies. Just four days after the attacks, sociologist Randal Collins and his team chose sites for geographical observation, at some geographical distance from the attack,[2] from which they could map and document the demonstrations of national solidarity, particularly the display of American flags (Collins, 2004). This research has demonstrated that the social practices in "reaction" to terrorist attacks cannot be best explained by the differential exposure of individuals to the "trauma," nor by their different political positions, but rather by their social and geographic situations.[3] There is an imitation effect too; individuals in isolated houses may not fly the flag as readily as those in high-density areas where flags are everywhere and there is an incitation to add one's own. Other studies have focused more specifically on the towns and neighborhoods that were physically targeted by the attacks, as was the case in Nancy Foner's investigation of several neighborhoods and social groups in New York, conducted between 2001 and 2003. Although it is entitled *Wounded City* (2005), the book that resulted from this research in fact distances itself from an exclusive approach in terms of collective trauma. Instead, it reveals the different ways in which the attacks have marked people depending on their sociological characteristics and social resources, with a tendency to reinforce pre-existing social differentiation.[4] In the wake of this collective research, Greg Smithsimon single-handedly conducted an in-depth three-year long study of the Battery Park City neighborhood near the World Trade Center, which was physically marked by

2   In neighborhoods in Philadelphia, San Diego, and Iowa city and rural towns in Maryland, Iowa and Virginia.

3   In addition to the chronicle "Seeing and being seen" in this book, a similar study was conducted in the French town of Brest in the wake of November 13, 2015 (Lagadec & *al.*, 2019).

4   For a summary of the results of this research see (Truc, 2019).

the collapse of the towers.[5] This neighborhood is home to a very socio-eco-nomically privileged population. As an urban sociologist, Smithsimon thus emphasizes the way in which the confrontation with "traumatic events" ultimately reinforced the community's existing closure onto itself, and thus intensified opposition against "others" (Smithsimon, 2011).

This book does not discuss 9/11, an extreme case if ever there was one (Tilly, 2004), if only because of the extent of urban destruction it involved (Sagalyn, 2016; Goldberger, 2005). It does however combine a focus on ordinary conversations and geographical observations to constitute a unique and unprecedented perspective on the memorialization of the 2015 terrorist attacks in Paris. It chronicles the day by day evolution of this memorialization in and around the Place de la République in Paris over the year that followed. This public square is a key site in both the history and geography of Paris; even today, this is where many popular demonstrations in the capital begin. At the center of the square there is a 9.5 m high bronze statue of Marianne, the female symbol of the French Republic, built in the 1880s. In her right hand, the statue holds aloft an olive branch, in her left, a tablet engraved with the declaration of human rights. The surrounding Place covers nearly 30,000 square meters and was renovated to be pedestrian-only in 2013. On January 7, 2015, the afternoon of the Charlie Hebdo shootings, the square was filled with people who came together to mourn the events that happened only a few blocks away. The base of the statue was immediately transformed into a gigantic grassroots memorial, that would remain in place until August 2016.

---

5   As I put the final touches to the manuscript of this book in November 2018, a mass-shooting has left 11 people dead at the Tree of Life Synagogue in Pittsburgh. The media documented the state of shock produced by this anti-Semitic attack, not just of the families and the religious community, but also of the residents in the neighborhood of Squirrel Hill, where the synagogue was. See, Bari Weiss, "When a Terrorist Comes to Your Hometown. The Jewish community center became a mourning tent. The synagogue, a crime scene" and "A massacre in the heart of Mr. Rogers's Neighborhood", *The New York Times*, respectively, November 2, and October 27, 2018. The community's struggle with this tragic event will undoubtedly give rise to future research.

Just ten months after January 2015, Paris was attacked again. The cafés targeted by the terrorists in the shootings on November 13, 2015 were in the 10th and 11th districts of the French capital and the Place de la République lies between these two areas. Once again it became the epicenter of commemorative events. The Bataclan concert hall, where ninety people were killed, is situated at number 50 Boulevard Voltaire, almost precisely between the Place and the Charlie Hebdo offices. I live on that same road with my partner and our two children, who were aged seven and four at the time of the attacks.

I am a sociologist of memory, specializing in qualitative and ethnographic research (Gensburger, 2020) and studying public policies of remembrance and their appropriations (Gensburger, 2016; Gensburger & Dybris McQuaid, 2019). By 2015, I had recently begun working on social memory and its localizations, using Paris as a site for my ethnographic fieldwork. One of my research projects at the time was studying the social uses of the more than 2000 commemorative plaques on display on the walls of the city, most of which refer to World War Two events (Gensburger & Lefranc, 2017). After the events of January, and especially November 2015, the phenomena that I was accustomed to studying in places and periods removed from my everyday life, were now unfolding in my own neighborhood, in the places that I visit every day. These places that my family and I passed on a daily basis became the stage for memorialization, for tributes and homages to the victims.

This personal and private experience prompted a new development in my memory research, which included a new form of sociological and public writing. For almost a year, I kept records and took notes on this memory process in the district. I decided to move away from the, then dominant, trauma-driven perspective by instead considering my neighborhood as a living place from which it was possible to pay attention to the social relationships people build with their environment, and to the role that environment plays in memory dynamics. In other words, I wanted to observe the streets and talk with people I met there, considering them as visitors and residents, rather than exclusively as victims confronted by the events. I began to write a sociological chronicle of my neighborhood, first on a daily basis and then weekly, paying attention to the urban and social spaces and linking my everyday life with my ethnographic work. I documented these chronicles with photographs I took of the area and the spaces people were investing with their memory. These sixty chronicles and more than one thousand pictures chart the impact of the events and the changes it provoked in the neighborhood from a perspective that is both personal and sociological. I published these texts and some of the photos, in French, on a blog which would become the core material of this book.[6] In this introduction, I want to briefly return to the experiment from a methodological perspective and to take stock of this day-to-day ethnographic field work.[7]

Part of this work can be described as autoethnographic. This technique was notably used by Carolyne Ellis to document the post-9/11 experiences of women in similar social positions to herself (2002). It is also worth noting that most autoethnographic studies have been conducted by female researchers, both on this theme and on others.[8] Following the pioneering work of Elizabeth Ettorre, I consider the idea of the self as an object of epistemological intrigue (2016). I therefore decided to situate a large part of my work within my everyday life, both as a Parisian and a mother. I also draw on the situationist methodology of John Urry (2007), and use notes from "genuine" ordinary conversations gleaned in my everyday interactions with family and friends, children's friends, neighbors, parents at school, teachers and shopkeepers, among others. Over the course of the year, I paid particular attention to when, and in which social situations, people from my life remembered and spoke, in one way or another, of and about the attacks. This methodology enabled me to grasp the vernacular memory of 11/13, at least in this particular group of residents of this area.

This epistemological choice also had ethical implications. Unlike what happens in the anglophone world, social science research in France does not have to be approved by a university ethics committee to proceed. However, I was attentive to two points in particular. Firstly, I made sure that the anonymity of anyone I spoke with was protected, even blurring faces in photos

---

6   The blog can be accessed at https://quartierdubataclan.wordpress.com. The photos and chronicles were published in the form of a book, in French (Gensburger, 2017). This English edition is the translation of these texts with a new introductory chapter and conclusion.

7   For an initial methodological review, of which this introduction is an additional step, see Gensburger, 2018a.

8   John Tulloch, media specialist, and victim of the 2005 London bombings, whose photograph was printed on the front page of the *Sun*, is an exception to this (2006).

when necessary. Secondly, I tried hard to find writing style that was as free as possible from any moral or judgmental perspectives, in order to really give a voice to everyone I interviewed, encountered, interacted with, or simply observed.

Beyond these ethical considerations, my methodological choices also had logistic implications. As Bernadette Barton (yet another female researcher) has clearly stated in relation to her autoethnographic research on her experience among the "Bible Belt gays," "almost every element of my life became 'data.' By this, I mean not only my daily lived experiences with my partner and [in her case gay] friends, but also my interactions with neighbors, students and colleagues. Among the many issues that have emerged during the course of this study is managing the volume of data I have collected" (2011, p. 432). This reflex of collecting conversations — even at the dinner table — has never left me. Since then it has spread to other themes, for example the experience of school groups (that my children are part of) participating in state commemorations for the centenary of the First World War, which, as I write in 2018, is now at its height.

However, the sociological chronicles published here do not rely exclusively on this autoethnographic approach. They also draw on more traditional methodologies. Between December 2015 and September 2016, I conducted around ninety field interviews with people at the site of grassroots memorials. When trying to engage people who stopped close to the site of the attacks, I often began with the introductory question "Do you often come to this part of Paris?" This question is slightly different from the ones regularly used by journalists and some colleagues studying these topics, such as "do you often come to mourn here?" or "did you lose someone in the attacks?", and this alternative formulation allowed me to collect slightly different material. This methodological framing meant that I could identify some of the commemorative practices I was observing as ordinary, often embedded in mundane acts of professional, economic and social mobility. Moreover, this methodological choice enabled the expression of multiple narratives around the event. These narratives were no longer limited to trauma and suffering, but also exposed how the site of a tragic event continued to function in its everyday, and socially differentiated, capacity (Heath-Kelly, 2016).

As well as engaging with people, both visitors and inhabitants, I also silently observed their behavior and above all listened to their conversations, because most of the people who stopped by the sites were not alone. These shared visits were silent at first, in keeping with ritualized mourning practices such as the "minute of silence" (Brown, 2012; Sánchez-Carretero, 2011). But observers also talked together, sometimes about what message they would write. Taking notes, and photos of these ordinary group interactions while observing the sites of the terrorist attacks enabled me to inscribe the messages left there within the group dynamics that led to their writing. Most of the written messages denounce the "horror" and express the writer's "pain" in an apparently consensual way. However, when we observe and listen to the group conversations that prompted these writings, it appears that the initial intentions were often far more controversial, political, and hotly debated (Antichan, 2016). For example, some writers may have at first planned to leave a message denouncing the participation of the French state in wars in the Middle East, or on the contrary, to stigmatize Muslims as an ethnic group. However, in most cases, the group dynamics I observed eventually led people to write a far more consensual message. They focused on praising peaceful coexistence or celebrating Paris. Here paying attention to ordinary conversations in the city allowed me to go far beyond the consensual surface of memorialization and its conceptualization as "resilient."

It quickly became apparent that what was at stake in most of the scenes I was observing were the differing interpretations of the events on the one hand, and the multiple pretentions of ownership over public space, on the other. In the chronicles that follow, the readers will discover many observations of this struggle over the appropriation of sites related to the attacks, their memorialization and the public reactions to them in the Parisian urban space.

One reason I was able to document this dimension was because, in addition to listening to conversations, drawing on field interviews and observations of memorial sites, I also used photography as a research tool (Fraenkel, 2002; Sturken, 2007). Since I was trying to pay attention to the mundane traces of memory in the public space, I immediately decided to take pictures of what I was seeing. This field practice provided the possibility to postpone the description and analysis of what I was seeing, and to return to it long after it had occurred. Using this method, I was able to document the tributes and commemorative material that had an ephemeral life in the streetscape. Moreover, the use of photography enabled me to construct a situated gaze on the memorialization of these attacks. As many colleagues have demonstrated (Pink, Sumartojo, Lupton & LaBond, 2017; Tolia-Kelly & Rose, 2012), photographs clearly constitute a very relevant material in working from a topographic perspective. Over the course of one year I took more than one thousand pictures. They helped me to keep track of things and served as a data resource through which I could filter my critical ethnographic analysis.

Indeed, overlapping with this analysis of memorialization was the progression of the Occupy movement in Paris. From March 31, 2016, the Place de la République was no longer exclusively a place for grassroots memorialization. It also became the hub of the social movement of occupation against the reform of labor laws in France; a movement that called itself "Nuit Debout" (the Night Rises). "Nuit Debout" marked a new stage in the dispute over public space, and it also revealed more broadly the fragmentation of the memory of the Paris attacks. Thanks to the photos I had taken, I was able to put this new protest movement over labor laws into a perspective with a topography of memory, "between social activism and commemoration" (Santino, 2011, p. 97). My use of photography as a research tool enabled me to trace a strong continuity between the memorialization of the attacks and the "Nuit Debout" movement, documenting how each social activity occupied different parts of the Place de la République, their temporal use of the space through the day, and the types of people involved. The side of the Place closest to the 11th district was always occupied by the protesters, from left-wing activists to advocates for international causes, and the other side, by representatives of state and its power, from policemen to the official "Memory Oak" inaugurated by the President in January 2016.

In addition, since my methodological starting point was not the 2016 social movement, but the physical site where it took place, I was able to make sense of the way in which other past events were evoked in the place de la République, including references to other terrorist attacks around the world, from Brussels to Orlando, but also references to the Paris Commune (the 1871 revolutionary movement), the First and Second World Wars, including the Collaboration by the French state, and also the figure of Anne Frank. The massacre of October 17, 1961 (when French police threw Algerian people protesting the Algerian war into the Seine River) and May 1968 were also mentioned. This photographic gaze led me to establish that the memorialization of the attacks was possibly conflictual and political rather than consensual and informed only by the shock of trauma. In more general, reciprocal terms, it provided a new perspective in confirming that memory issues play a significant and dynamic role in contemporary political debates and in the public forum of French contemporary society. References to resilience sometimes "conceal all the microcosms and complex politics of the event" (Heath-Kelly, 2017).

Finally, putting this research experimentation into practice was facilitated by the fact that, being the mother of two young children, my son and daughter accompanied me for much of the fieldwork. Some recent studies have taken stock of the methodological benefits and limitations of involving children in ethnography (Allerton, 2016). In my case, it was not a conscious choice but more of a secondary consequence of my decision to embed this research in my everyday life. At first, the presence of my children seemed a burden rather than a benefit. When I was in the field, I had to keep one eye on them as well as on my observations and do the "care-work" Danielle Drozdzewski and Daniel. F. Robinson describe in their personal reflections on their own experience with children (2015). I initially felt that I was not fully available to conduct the observation as I would have liked because they were with me. However, my children's presence turned out to be very fruitful. They ended up participating fully in the study.

Indeed, as Greg Smithsimon experienced in his own fieldwork at Battery Park, having children can help facilitate contact with strangers (2011). But, more importantly, their views were very helpful because of the way children tend to "normalize" what they see, including when they are faced with violence (Dygregnov and al., 2016). Drawing on her experience with primary school children in Argentina, Diana Milstein says, for example, children's "views provided distance from what one could term the 'official conscience' pervading adult opinion. This distance was possible, among other reasons, because the children had not completely incorporated some of the conventions that made up adult discourse in a certain time and place" (2010: 1). Indeed, children, especially young children like mine, are likely to express differently socialized and framed opinions and feelings. Refracting these everyday scenes through the eyes of my daughter and son helped me connect with the everyday setting and remove the more immediate tendency I had, as a sociologist, to focus on an exclusively traumatic reading of the attacks and their aftermath. Several of my children's remarks and reactions resonated strongly with me. On many occasions, for them, making sense of the most dramatic events relied on very mundane social habits. My memories of them witnessing and processing the social interactions in our neighborhood meant that the everydayness of method became even more salient for me.

References to the attacks and remembrance of it were contingent on the social situations my children were in. My son, for example, apparently considers police officers, tourists, and journalists to be ordinary figures on our streets now; this new face of our neighborhood since November 2015 has become completely "normal" for him. For example, and as the reader will discover in some of the following pages, on Saturday June 4, 2016, we were waiting for the "Tropical Carnival" parade, which is supposed to come down the Boulevard du Temple, one street away from ours coming from the Place de la République. Originally created by the Caribbean community in Paris to showcase their heritage, the carnival has in recent years included many cultures from all around the world. At the head of the parade, for security reasons that were obvious to me, there were around thirty police officers in combat uniform. My son turned toward me with a huge smile and said *"Maman*, you didn't say there'd be a police carnival too! That's so cool!". In his eyes the social situation was quite distinct from and without reference to the attacks. However, a year later, in December 2017, he evoked the memory of the attack very clearly while playing Monopoly with his sister and me. He was looking for a situation where someone could leave the game without losing, so that he could keep playing with his sister (according to the rules, my bankruptcy should have brought an end to the game). He clearly mobilized the reference to the terrorist attacks, saying to me "imagine that you were killed in an attack in the street — then you would be out of the game!" (without being bankrupt). Beyond the dichotomy between trauma and resilience, and between forgetting and memory, for my kids, as well as for other people I speak with in my everyday life, there are social situations and interactions in which it is meaningful to recall the attacks and other where it is not.

In other words, researching memory on my doorstep meant shedding light on the existence of social continuity, beyond the rupture created by the violence of the event, and stressing the fact that this continuity, too, participated in the social frameworks in which the memory of the event has taken form. Ten years after 9/11, Joshua Woods used large-scale survey data to ask "was America 'a country united' after 9/11?" before concluding that "according to social scientists, the answer is yes and no" (2012, p. 42). However, if we were to ask, "is France a united country after November 13," based on the research in this book, it is necessary to reformulate the question. Instead, we should ask, "who reacted to the event, how, when, and in what situation(s)?" and "how do individuals, in their different social situations, remember and discuss it?"

Of course, autoethnography (Delamont, 2009), or even ethnography (Truc, 2019), are not enough to provide systematic answers to these questions. The results of a questionnaire-based survey on the memorialization of the November 13 attacks, conducted with a representative sample of the French population (Hoibian et al., 2018), already provides a useful perspective on the field data published in this book. It emphasizes to what extent the attacks in Paris left a mark on many people in France. But at the same time, it also shows how the most disadvantaged socio-economic categories (low income and insecure employment situations) seem to be less concerned by the memory of the events than the population as a whole, and particularly so when compared to more privileged social groups. Conversely, this study shows that young adults aged between 25 and 39 years old — the age group of most of the victims of November 13 — seem to carry their memory more than others. In addition to a reading structured around trauma, as justified and important as that is, understanding the memory of these attacks also means identifying their social frameworks (Halbwachs, 1925) and their situations of enunciation (Pollak, 1993). This must be done far from the too often sterile oppositions between memory and forgetting (Connerton, 2008, Draaisma, 2015) or between public and private space (Doss, 2010).

On Saturday January 7, 2017, my son invited a dozen of his friends to our home on Boulevard Voltaire, one block from the place de la République. It was a somewhat belated party for his fifth birthday. Several children arrived late. "So, sorry, there's another demonstration at République," the parents said, one by one. "The neighborhood is blocked off, I don't know what's going on." "There's something organized on the square." It was two years to the day since the shooting at Charlie Hebdo had taken place just streets away from my house. The police had set up roadblocks so that a commemorative ceremony could be held, organized by the French Association for Victims of Terrorism. Not one of my visitors seemed to see the significance of the date or make the connection with the traffic problems — which have been systematic whenever there is an official anniversary or a state visit in this part of the 11th district over the last two years.

We might conclude that the residents of the neighborhood have repressed the events that took place on their doorsteps, extra proof of the collective trauma produced by the attacks of January and November 2015. We might also hypothesize that there are social situations that are more conducive to reliving the emotion of this violent past, and others that are less so, or which might even make such social evocations of it impossible or insignificant, without necessarily involving repression. There is also a third hypothesis. There is no shared commemorative calendar or collective interpretation of these events. The fact that commemorations were held every day in the neighborhood between Thursday 5 and Sunday 8 January 2017, organized by various political figures or community actors, resulted in a kind of dilution of the temporal anchorage and signification of remembrance for those living in the area. For them, these repeated ceremonies came to be part of the everyday streetscape. They attended them inadvertently, on the way to the bakery, or taking the children to school.

The chronicles published in this book aim to explore the coexistence of these different dynamics at work in the construction of the memory of the 2015 terrorist attacks in Paris.[9]

---

9 I made the decision to publish the chronicles as they were written, as a way of documenting the research process as it happened, with the hope that they might be used in the teaching of sociological methods. In addition to this introductory chapter, which is both theoretical and methodological, a concluding chapter has also been added to look more closely at the book's contribution to memory studies, to engage with the most recent scientific literature as well as to retrace what has become of the memorialization of the 2015 Paris attacks since I finished writing these chronicles.

Paris, 11th arrondissement, Boulevard Voltaire

December 27, 2015 — September 20, 2016

I live halfway between the Place de la République and the Bataclan concert hall.

On November 13, my partner, my two young children and I returned home about 9 pm. My son and my daughter were both asleep when the shootings began. At first, we adults heard nothing. And then the deafening sounds of sirens and the avalanche of telephone calls. A night without sleep. A night that was the same for all the residents in our neighborhood. And then the day that came after. There was nothing special about our experience, probably nothing worth writing about.

It is what happened afterwards, once the event itself was "over," that is the subject of this book and these observations of memory on my doorstep.

I am a sociologist. As a researcher I specialize in social memory and its localizations, and for several years I have been studying the city of Paris as my primary field site. Of course, these two facts are not enough to explain who I am, but they do help to describe the position from which I am writing.

These texts are not intended to be a diary. They are provoked by the fact that social phenomena which I am used to studying in other places and periods, are now unfolding in my own neighborhood, on my doorstep.

As a sociologist, these texts are a way of sharing my own process of understanding. As a resident of the 11th arrondissement,[1] they are a way for me to

---

1   This arrondissement is home to nearly 150 000 residents according to the latest census.

put some distance between myself and my immediate environment, which has become sometimes difficult to deal with since the attacks.

These chronicles are thus situated at the crossroads of these two worlds. Written day by day, in this space that had brutally become so specific, they were also cathartic for me.

Yet they have still another function. Backed by a sociological approach of distancing myself from my research object, they also fulfill my long-felt need to establish a form of narration that is different from those of academic studies.

Sociologists, historians, political scientists and other anthropologists reformulate the questions that society poses about itself, and sometimes they are able to answer them. One of the lessons from the attacks that have touched France since 2015 is that their studies are often not widely known. They rarely inspire political or non-governmental actors and are frequently unable to make their findings available for those who are the object of this research. Moreover, they generally fail to promote alternative understandings of the world, and to reveal it in ways other than through the immediacy of experiences.

In these chronicles I wanted to think aloud. Each text renders the rhythm, the meanderings, and sometimes the wrong turns of my approach. They ask the reader to follow me, in the hope that he or she might also take a look at society with his or her eyes wide open.

These chronicles rely heavily on photography, traveling as they do through time and space. Intrinsically connected to the text, these photographs provide a visual narrative, which sometimes says more, and sometimes speaks differently from the text itself. They contribute to the book's goal of proposing a situated gaze on the memorialization of these attacks in the space of the city. Fueled by analysis and observations, impressions and uncertainties, this atypical book has another final reason for being: it aims to encourage others to look upon what I have seen, to see something else, to understand things differently and, above all, to ask (themselves) questions, forever and everywhere.

Bd Magenta

10e

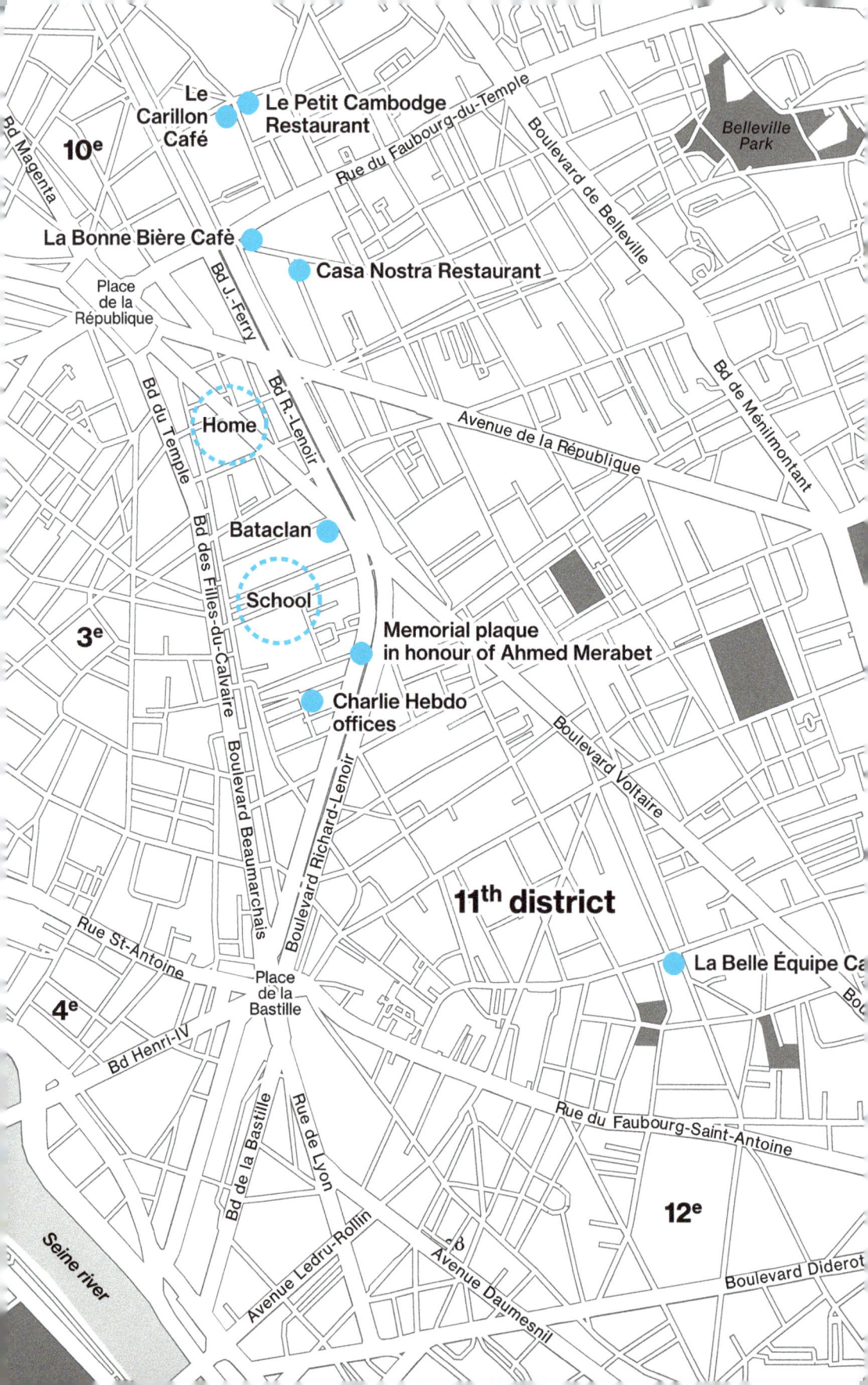

Le Carillon Café

Le Petit Cambodge Restaurant

Rue du Faubourg-du-Temple

Boulevard de Belleville

Belleville Park

La Bonne Bière Cafè

Bd J.-Ferry

Casa Nostra Restaurant

Place de la République

Bd du Temple

Bd R.-Lenoir

Avenue de la République

Bd de Ménilmontant

Home

Bataclan

Bd des Filles-du-Calvaire

School

Memorial plaque in honour of Ahmed Merabet

3e

Charlie Hebdo offices

Boulevard Richard-Lenoir

Boulevard Beaumarchais

Boulevard Voltaire

11th district

Rue St-Antoine

La Belle Équipe Ca

4e

Place de la Bastille

Bd Henri-IV

Bd de la Bastille

Rue de Lyon

Rue du Faubourg-Saint-Antoine

12e

Avenue Ledru-Rollin

Avenue Daumesnil

Boulevard Diderot

Seine river

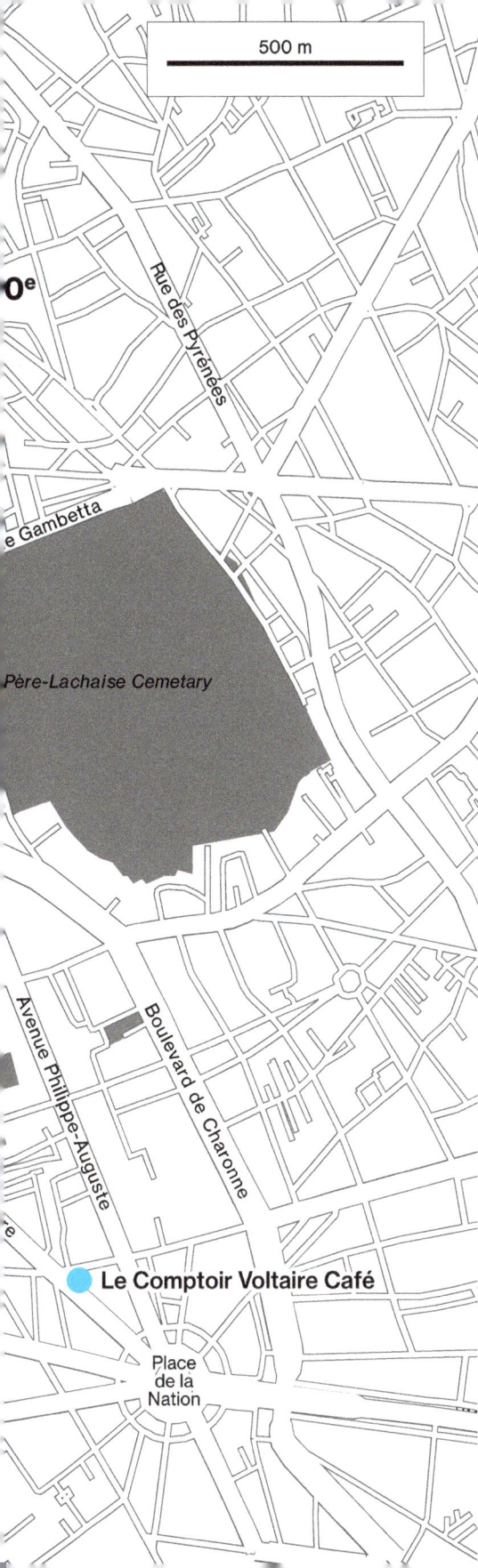

500 m

10e

Rue des Pyrénées

e Gambetta

Père-Lachaise Cemetary

Avenue Philippe-Auguste

Boulevard de Charonne

e

Le Comptoir Voltaire Café

Place
de la
Nation

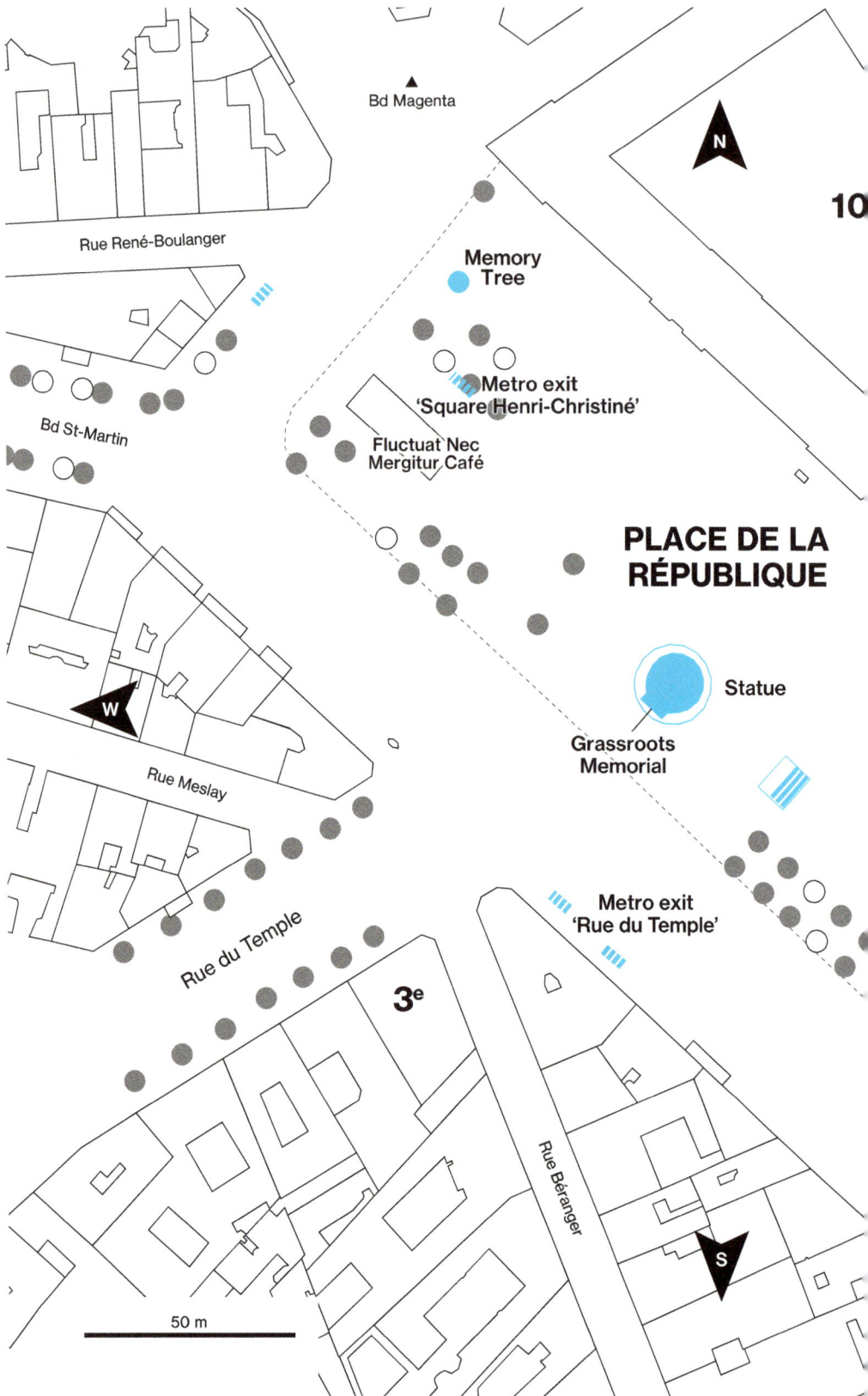

Bd Magenta

N

10

Rue René-Boulanger

Memory
Tree

Bd St-Martin

Metro exit
'Square Henri-Christiné'

Fluctuat Nec
Mergitur Café

PLACE DE LA
RÉPUBLIQUE

W

Statue

Rue Meslay

Grassroots
Memorial

Rue du Temple

Metro exit
'Rue du Temple'

3e

Rue Béranger

S

50 m

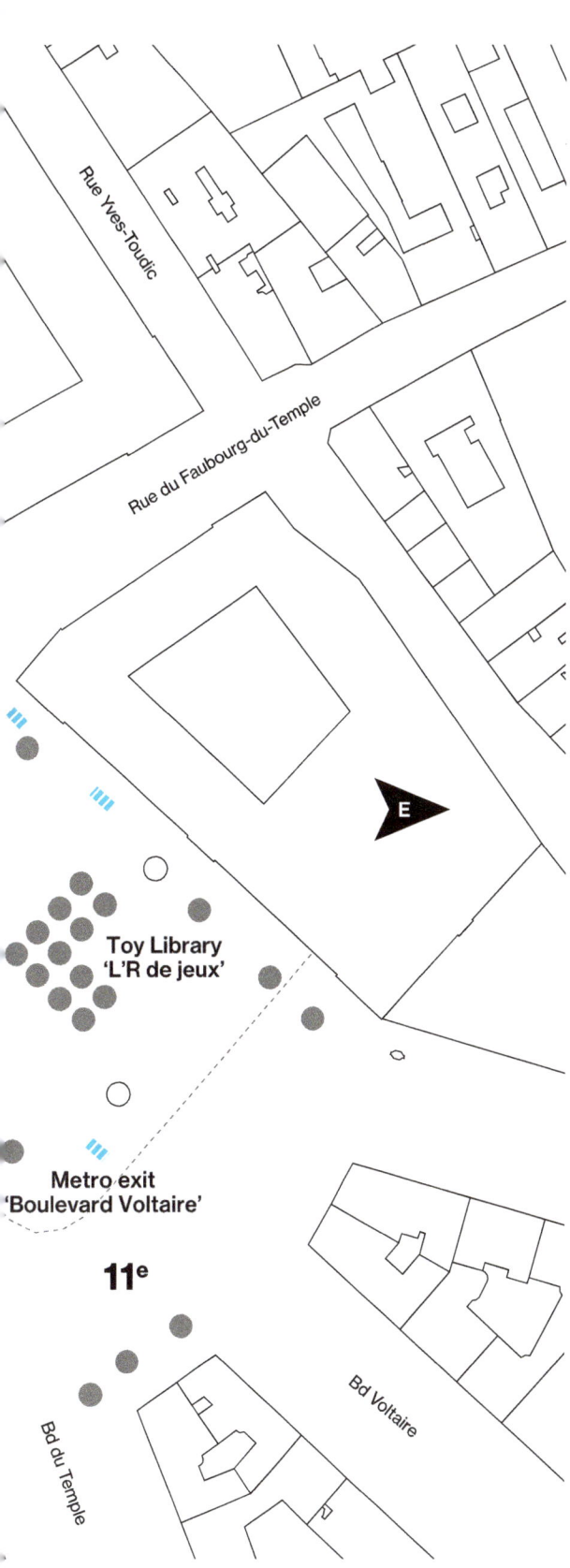

Rue Yves-Toudic

Rue du Faubourg-du-Temple

E

**Toy Library
'L'R de jeux'**

**Metro exit
'Boulevard Voltaire'**

11e

Bd Voltaire

Bd du Temple

Event(s)

December 27, 2015

On Sunday December 27, at around 10.30am I left home with my seven-year-old daughter. Often when we go out running together on the weekend, my daughter asks to run past her school. Like every morning and evening during term-time, we went past the Bataclan concert hall, which is on our way to her school. Today, for the first time since the shootings, we were able to walk along the footpath in front of the Bataclan. The two gray tarpaulins and the police van had gone. The flowers, candles, texts, objects and other offerings had also disappeared. Being able to stay on the footpath, and keep running, was for us an event in itself.

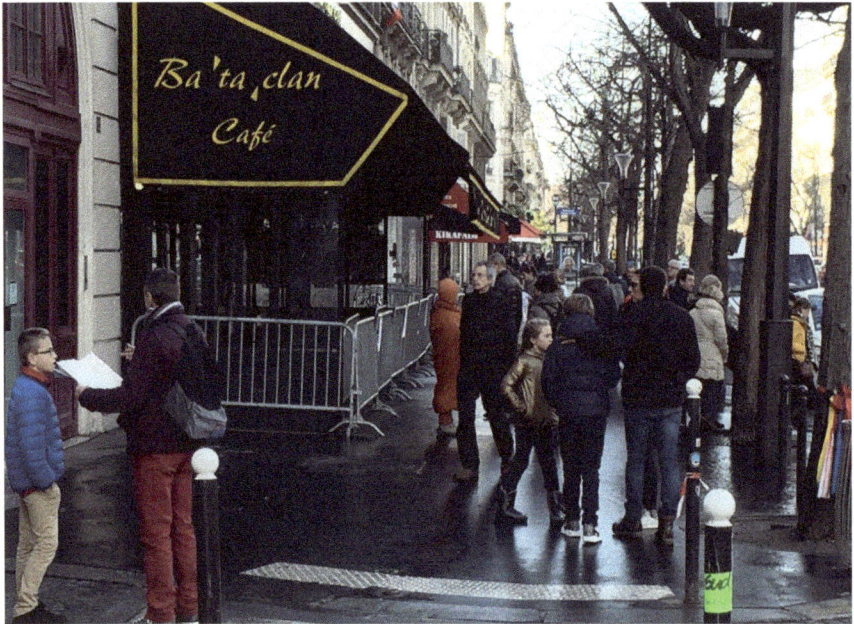

ʌ In front of the Bataclan café, December 27, 2015, around 10.30 am.

A The same place (from a different viewpoint, the previous one being then inaccessible), photographed on December 8, 2015, around 10 am, from the sidewalk on Boulevard Richard Lenoir, across the road from the Bataclan.

The feeling of liberation that I felt, and which I freely recognized as somewhat ridiculous, made me want to stop running and look at the footpath and the surroundings. It was not the first time since the massacre that I had looked in this way, but it was the first time that I was able to do so without anger and exhaustion. This experience, this lived event, was the point of origin for these chronicles.

There can be no doubt that the attacks in Paris on November 13 constitute an "event," such as historians consider essential in the analysis of social and political transformations. Yet, as social science has demonstrated, the event is always subjectively interpreted and the very idea that an event can exist collectively must be considered with caution.

In the case of September 11, for example, one of the ways of trying to understand the effects of the event consists in studying not how individuals remember it directly, but how they remember the context in which they first heard about it (with whom, where, doing what etc.) (Hirst and al., 2015; Luminet & Curci, 2017). It is through these *flashbulb memories*, and not in itself that an event is remembered. When I think of the night of November 13, it is also this other "event," this banal outing with my daughter two weeks after the actual event, which is meaningful for me.

Distance

December 28, 2015

I have apparently become a "resident of the Bataclan district." The media has coined the term to account — only partially but rightly nonetheless — for the difficulty living here, in an environment that that is continually made morbid by the numerous tributes in the public space.

Naturally, it is more complicated than that. There is also a form of courage that residents draw on in the face of adversity, and which they have drawn on again for the second time in just a few months. And the feeling of being "residents of the Bataclan district" is not as straightforward as that. Have we stopped being "Charlie's neighbors," to use the terms of a local organization set up in the wake of the attack in January 2015?[1] Can we be residents of several districts at once?

Regaining access to the sidewalk was an important moment, but it is not going to make us forget the dead, or to stop the flow of visitors gathering in memory. But by allowing us to walk, to gather and to park around the Bataclan once again, restoring residents their habitual use of their neighborhood, it also allows us to think upon the personal relations we maintain with the space in which we live, the city, its roads and buildings. Maurice Halbwachs, whose research on collective memory has been an important resource for me over the years, emphasizes the extent to which society is structured in its connections to the physical space:

1   See the chronicle "Neighbors", March 1, 2016.

"Society is embedded in a material world, and collective thought finds, in the representations that are transmitted through these spatial conditions, a principle for regularity and stability, just as individual thought must perceive body and space in order to maintain its balance." (Halbwachs, 1938, p. 18).

In the wake of the attacks, the "neighborhood" now reveals new "spatial conditions" to those who live in it. And from them, this disturbance in habitual things, is born the possibility of examining what is happening, not only as a resident but also as a sociologist. Indeed, it is not "neutrality" (as the general public often believes) that allows an individual to take other individuals as research objects. It is the creation of distance, the permanent shifting of gaze, and the constant changes in perspective.

Traces

December 30, 2015

▲ Photograph taken Place de la République, on December 28, 2015, around 5.15 pm. Out of respect for the anonymity of those in the photo I have concealed their faces. Here they are like all the other "characters" in these chronicles. The objective is not to refer to people in particular but to think about the ways in which memorialization establishes itself in the public space.

On Monday December 28, my daughter and I come home on the metro. We get off at République station and take an exit that means we have to walk across the square. For a long time now, since well before the "events," my daughter has considered the statue on the Place de la République to be somehow hers. Her second name is Marianne.

She looks closely at it, as she always does:

"Oh there's lots more people than usual. There was almost no one last time."

We come here often, this is our home.

"It's the school holidays, you know, maybe there are a lot of tourists," I replied.

We observe an argument between a man standing on the base of the statue, his hands full of papers, and a woman perched on a bicycle. The two seem to be around sixty years old and they are talking about what the man is in the process of doing. He has picked up some of the papers and letters, left there in tribute by passersby.

"You're not allowed to, it's not up to you," says the woman.

"I'm not taking them. I'm going to laminate them, to protect them," replies the man.

"If people put them there like that then that's their right. And it's not a problem that they get damaged, or destroyed. I like it when the flowers fade," the woman insists.

"But people didn't think to laminate them, of course, they're very emotional. We'll laminate them so that they last."

I ask him who is the "we" he refers to, and he says, "I'm with a group that aims to pay homage to the victims and preserve the homages people have paid to them."

What traces are left by these events? To whom do these traces belong?

Trace

December 31, 2015

A few days before the beginning of the school holidays, the Paris Archives provided the beginning of an answer to the question left hanging at the end of the previous chronicle. On several occasions, archival staff have come to sort through and preserve the texts and objects left in homage in front of the Bataclan since November 13.[1] It is partly thanks to them that I have regained access to the sidewalk.

On the sidewalk outside the Bataclan there are still metal barriers to prevent people from getting too close. Attached to the barriers is an official statement from the 11th District Council, explaining what has happened to all the tributes left there.

A single trace has replaced the many traces. My repeated observations of this space, conducted since December 26, suggest that visitors read this municipal statement with as much solemnity as they do with the messages and tributes that continue to be left on the footpath across the road, along the side of the park on Boulevard Richard Lenoir.

Here, a statement about the destiny of the traces has itself become a trace, a sign that something happened here.

[1] Before August 1, 2016 this archival collection never included the documents and objects left at the base of the statue on Place de la République, several chronicles will discuss this.

"To all concerned,

In the wake of the tragic events of November 13, many of you have expressed your solidarity and paid tribute to the victims of the attacks. Many objects, flowers, candles and messages have been left at the sites of the places touched by these events.

It is now necessary to reconcile each person's need for commemoration and remembrance while guaranteeing the residents of this area a calmer living environment, after these tragic events that caused profound upheaval in the life of the neighborhood.

We therefore inform you that the City municipal services intervened here on the morning of Tuesday December 22. All tributes left here from as early as Saturday November 14, have been moved along the side of the park on Boulevard Richard Lenoir.

This operation, conducted in the strictest respect for the tributes left, was performed by the staff of the Paris Archive, accompanied by the City street cleaning staff. The objects and messages that must be removed because they are damaged will be preserved in the City Archives. Concerning the flowers and candles, the City staff will remove only those which are damaged.

Moreover, Paris City Council has launched a photographic campaign to document all the tributes, under the scientific supervision of the Departmental Archives Services. The City has also opened a platform on its website, Paris.fr to display the tributes published on social networks using the hashtag #NousSommesUnis [we are one], the emails received by the City services, and the messages of support received by other cities and towns in France and overseas."

∧ Extract from the monumental fresco that covered Boulevard Richard Lenoir on November 16, 2015. "One for all Paris"; "The Republic is not dead."

Disappearance
January 1, 2016

Who can legitimately look after these tributes? Whose responsibility is it to preserve them?

Is a residents' group responsible for maintaining the tributes on the Place de la République? Are the Paris Archives responsible for those outside the Bataclan?

Although important, this question must necessarily be asked in vain. In spite of the efforts to preserve them, these traces are also destined to disappear.

On Monday November 16, after dropping off my children at school, I walked along the Boulevard Richard Lenoir. The ground was covered by a giant chalk fresco done by street artists and I had a feeling of wonder, walking on this artistic abundance. It was almost as though the splendor of the ceiling of the Opéra Garnier, painted by Chagall, had come to decorate what we ordinarily think of as just the "median strip" behind our building. These chalk drawings were quickly washed away. Today only journalistic records and photographs remain.

What should be preserved? Gérôme Truc, a colleague of mine, wrote an insightful thesis on the reactions provoked by the terrorist attacks in Madrid, London and New York. Today he rightly wants to undertake the same kind of investigation into the situation in Paris (Truc, 2018 [2016]). The search is overwhelming, how can nothing be left behind? Collecting tweets, reaping the content of websites, observing the space of the city, analyzing archives, and so on: it is impossible to give a voice to those traces that have already disappeared. And the selection of the traces to be studied will influence the results of any research.

Appearance

January 4, 2016

There is also a temptation to interpret any change in the landscape of the neighborhood in light of November 13. The meaning of the physical traces left by the events resides largely in the way these traces are perceived and interpreted.

I took this photograph on November 25, 2015 on Boulevard Voltaire. At the time, even though the neighborhood was still covered with all sorts of tributes and objects, it seemed obvious to me that this bright pink magic wand conveyed its own message — one of optimism.

Today, with hindsight, I cannot ignore the possibility that this magic wand was simply lost by a child in the street and stuck to the pole by a well-meaning passerby. Just like the lost gloves or scarves we often see draped over the railings of the park in winter, in case their former owners retrace their steps to find them.

But what about the branch attached to the wand? At the time, I took it to be an olive branch, a symbol of peace, a message attached to a found object.

I looked on Google images to see if the author of this tribute had posted a photo somewhere of his or her creation, but to no avail. The image recognition program matched the wand with a set of traffic lights in London...[1]

This experience of possible over-interpretation of the transformations of the neighborhood illustrates one of John Urry's conclusions (2002), in his study of the "tourist gaze." Observing the traces of the past, and the space around oneself more broadly, is always an activity that is framed and structured by a pre-existing familiarity with other images. When this photograph was taken, I was so accustomed to encountering tributes and homages in the neighborhood, that this encouraged me to interpret every unexpected object through this analytic frame.

The decision to write these personal chronicles, from a perspective which ultimately remains scientific, is what has enabled me to distance myself from this wand-tribute and consider the limits of my initial interpretation.

1   http://hidden-london.com/gazetteer/wimpole-street/

Plaques

January 5, 2016

From as early as December 19, the residents of our neighborhood were
informed that on January 5 there may be disruptions to traffic due to the
presence of the President of the Republic and the Mayor of Paris for the
inauguration of the commemorative plaques in honor of the victims of the
Charlie Hebdo shootings, which took place here last January.[1]

1   One plaque was inaugurated outside 10 rue rue Nicolas Appert, in homage to
the people killed during the attack on Charlie Hebdo on January 7. A second
was erected outside 62 boulevard Richard Lenoir in memory of Ahmed Merabet,
the policeman killed as the attackers fled.

But once the inauguration was over, once the spelling mistake had been corrected,[2] would passersby stop to read the plaques? What uses would Parisians and tourists make of these different places that have been called "sites of memory?"

Both in France and elsewhere, various studies have looked at the attitudes of passersby to the urban heritage that surrounds them. These studies primarily focus on the origins of this material, the way the past is evoked, or the semiotic interpretations of their forms and content. Very few have really looked at the question of how the people navigating a city actually interact with these plaques.

In Paris, there are lots of commemorative plaques. They pay homage to famous authors, to Resistance fighters, to politicians, or to artists. In this respect, the inauguration taking place this morning is another confirmation that the City of Paris has long considered erecting plaques to be its preferred instrument of memory policy.

Most of the plaques in Paris are in reference to the Second World War. The Paris Council has made data available, as part of its open data policy, that allow us to locate and number this particular subcategory of plaques: in 2014, there were 1300 plaques relating to this war. In the 11th arrondissement alone there are eighty-seven plaques commemorating this period, making this neighborhood one of the most densely covered of the city. It therefore seems illusionary to suppose that Parisians — or even tourists — pay any real attention to these reminders of the past, which are far too

---

2   On January 5, 2016, the media coverage of the inauguration of the plaque in homage to the people killed at Charlie Hebdo was marked by controversy over a spelling mistake in one of the victims' names, incorrectly spelt Georges Wolinksy, instead of Wolinski.

numerous for a single individual to take in. Yet, from time to time, tributes or flowers added to some of these plaques show that someone has noticed them, or has, in one way or another, appropriated them.

⋏ This photograph was taken 2 bis Rue de Lyon in the 12th arrondissement. Someone has written in pen "Some flowers please" (in French). On this day, the City Council did in fact leave flowers, as a one-time gesture, because it was the 72nd anniversary of the liberation of Paris.

This observation, made between 2014 and 2015, in the context of my new research project on the localization of memory, led me to become interested in the plaques not for themselves and their text, but for their situation, context and possible interactions with the city and its passersby.[3] Between March and July 2014, I conducted a study on this, in collaboration with Micol Bez, who is a student from Georgetown University and a great lover of Paris, and also with my students from the Institute for French Studies at

3   For more on this research, see the introduction of the book.

New York University, who I took with me to discover the city. We repeatedly and systematically observed roughly forty plaques in different areas of Paris.

Among the plaques in our corpus was the one commemorating the anti-Semitic attack from 1982, in which gunmen opened fire in a crowded room of the "Jo Goldenberg" restaurant in the Rue des Rosiers, killing several customers.

Having disappeared for a time, this plaque was put up again in 2011 by the Paris City Council on the façade of the restaurant, which is now a clothes shop. Like those put up on January 5 to commemorate the Charlie Hebdo shooting, it lists the names of the victims and the precise circumstances of the killing. During our study, we observed that only a very small number of passersby stopped to look at it, and among those that did, very few actually read the inscription.

Moreover, during the informal interviews we conducted afterwards with more than a dozen members of the neighborhood (residents, restaurant owners, shopkeepers etc.) these events were not mentioned. Although all of them had noticed that there was a plaque here, some had nothing at all to say about it and most were convinced that it was to commemorate the Jewish people who were killed during the Second World War.[4]

This empirical observation cannot be generalized, however. It does not mean that commemorative plaques are useless. Rather it should encourage us to reformulate the questions that we ask about them and the kind of answers we expect to receive.

4   However, when they were questioned about it at the end of the interview, most people did in fact know that there had been an attack here.

Gazes

January 6, 2016

This afternoon I went to observe the area around the two plaques erected yesterday in the neighborhood, for half an hour each. Of course, no statistical conclusions can be drawn from these observations, but they do provide clues that may be read in light of the existing research.

On Boulevard Richard Lenoir, roughly one hundred people passed by the plaque in memory to Ahmed Merabet, the policeman killed in this very same street a few minutes after the Charlie Hebdo shooting. More than two thirds of them stopped to look at it, and in general they took the time to read it and take in the space.

On Rue Nicolas Appert, in front of the Charlie Hebdo offices, there were half as many passersby over the same amount of time. Only a small minority of them actually looked at the plaque and those who did so glanced at it only briefly.

I saw one man at both sites; he had clearly come to look, in detail, at the two plaques. But he was the only one, if we don't count the few journalists who were there to collect images.

Are people more "interested" in the fate of Ahmed Merabet than that of the other victims of January 2015? Framed in these terms the question answers itself. However, here we are interested in investigating these modest clues in a different way.

◄ Passersby in front of the plaque on Boulevard Richard Lenoir.

Although no large-scale ethnographic study has been conducted on the people who visit the city through its commemorative plaques, this is not the case for those who visit its museums. These onlookers, who become "visitors," have been studied from almost every possible angle (McDonald, 2006). This research has clearly established that the visitors' experiences of exhibitions are framed by the physical possibilities of moving around the museum — such as the size of the rooms, the crowds, the width of the corridors, or the height at which the works are hung. The act of visiting a museum is also, and sometimes even primarily, a spatial experience.

We can also apply this framework for analysis to those who visit memorial sites in public spaces. It is therefore possible to examine several key differences between the two plaques inaugurated in the neighborhood. Firstly, it is important to realize that the Boulevard Richard Lenoir is a very busy street, for cyclists as well as pedestrians. This is not the case for the Rue Nicolas Appert, which is a short residential backstreet, leading to no major road. Secondly, the plaque to the memory of Ahmed Merabet is situated at eye level while that for the victims at Charlie Hebdo's offices is placed much higher on the wall, which creates a certain distance that is less conducive to empathy.

Of course this material reading of the visitor's gaze is not sufficient in itself: homage to a single person on one hand, or to a group of people on the other, may not encourage the same degree of identification with the victims. Moreover, Ahmed Merabet's ethnic and religious background has led some to consider his fate particularly exemplary[1]. On one hand this may appear banal, but it is an important reminder that in terms of commemoration, the effects produced — which still need to be demonstrated and studied — may not stem solely from the past evoked, or from the words used to narrate them, but also from spatial and material factors.

---

1   Merabet was born in a family of Algerian origin and his death fighting against the Islamist Charlie Hebdo attackers was seen by certain commentators as an illustration of "republican values".

Interpretation
January 8, 2016

It is very difficult for observers, even researchers, to grasp the meaning of commemorative practices. What are the paths (figurative and literal) that bring visitors to the scene of these attacks, and why? What meaning(s) do these visitors invest in the words, photos, objects and flags that they leave there?

In the wake of September 11, slogans and writings progressively appeared on walls around New York. These "September writings" — as Béatrice Faenkel called them — gave rise to several fascinating analyses, of their contents, and more rarely, of their spatial organization (Fraenkel, 2002). The study of the visitors' books filled in at exhibitions have indeed shown that the messages that people leave are greatly influenced by what others have written (McDonald, 2005).

These textual and spatial approaches are limited, however, when it comes to retracing the sources and means of this commemoration — it is impossible to identify who left a particular "tribute." Naming, and thus describing, what is left in the city space in reaction to the attacks already constitutes an act of interpretation for which the researcher has little data to rely on. What do these "things," left on the footpath in front of the Bataclan since November 13, actually constitute?

On January 5, four of my colleagues agreed to accompany me to observe the intersection between Boulevard Richard Lenoir and Boulevard Voltaire.[1] Some of us were to draw an overall portrait of visitors according to gender,

---

1 A warm thank you to these colleagues: Sylvain Antichan, Brian Chauvel, Julie Lavielle and Brett Le Saint.

PARIS NOVEMBER 13, 2015

IN HONOR OF THE MARTYRS
VICTIMS OF THE BARBARITY OF
DAESH (IS) EXTREMISTS

WE WILL NEVER FORGET THEM
AND THEY WILL REMAIN FOREVER
IN OUR HEARTS

residency, age or attitudes, between quickly taking photographs and carefully reading all the tributes. My other colleagues were to spend their time talking to particular individuals. We were there for one hour, during which four "offerings" were added, three bunches of flowers and one text. This text was already laminated, and its author visibly meant it to last and be preserved.

My colleague, Brian Chauvel took the opportunity to engage this person in an informal conversation. The genealogy of this text will therefore be recorded for the future when the text ultimately ends up among the documents from the grassroots memorial collected by the Paris Archives.

◄ This text was printed on an A4 sheet of paper and left at 12.20pm on January 5, 2016 by a man who walked with some difficulty, using a cane. He left it after several attempts to find a place for it on the fence around the park on Boulevard Richard Lenoir. He said that he was a retired postal worker from Paris, now living in the Creuse region in the south of France. He said that this was his first visit to Paris since November 2015. He had come in the company of an old colleague who was accustomed to bringing his visitors to the scene of the attacks, and who had himself lost a close friend at the Bataclan.

Photography

January 9, 2016

All interpretations are based on materials, on gestures and actions observed, and on words that are heard. These materials depend as much on the questions that we ask ourselves as they do on the questions we ask others.

This morning, on the Boulevard Richard Lenoir, a visitor was taking photographs of the flowers and the messages. A journalist approached him and asked "Could you tell me why you have come to pay homage at scene of the attacks?" The man accepted the terms of this dialog and responded politely to the question he was asked. But my colleague Jeanne Teboul, who was also present, immediately wondered aloud — to what extent is photographing the tributes the same as "paying homage?"

Since November 13, photography has had an important role in the relation people have with the scenes of these attacks. Visitors come and take photos. This is the same practice as in museums. Chloé Roubert for example has shown how the Rosetta Stone, displayed in the British Museum, existed firstly through the photos that were taken of it and reproduced (Roubert, 2011).

Far from an act of homage, this practice is firstly a way for the visitor to appropriate the subject of the photo — whether they are archeological remains, or homages to victims of terrorism. Photography is a testimony to one's presence in a particular place. And the ways in which it is done can be far removed from those that we habitually expect from a space of remembrance. Although selfies are rare on the Boulevard Richard Lenoir, they are more frequent on the Passage Saint-Pierre-Amelot, where the emergency exit from the Bataclan comes out.[1] The walls of this street are marked with several bullet marks and it is not unusual to see people use them as a backdrop in their portraits.

"Could you tell me why you have come to pay homage at the scene of the attacks?" This could be a question framed by a researcher. But it would have been poorly framed, because it traps the dialog that it seeks to elicit in preconceptions that prevent any new discovery. Students of sociology are advised to formulate their questions in such a way as to base the conversation on individual's concrete practices — in other words to start with themselves and their conceptions. "When?", "what?", and "with whom?" should be used rather than "how?", "why?" and "what for?"

Indeed, discussing concrete practices tends to elicit the values and beliefs of an individual more readily than if these had been questioned directly, like an instruction to accept or to believe. However, even once this principle has been established, it remains a delicate task to undertake. For several days now, my colleagues and I have been looking for an acceptable way to approach the visitors. "Is this the first time you have come here?" is, for the moment, our invitation to dialog.

1 The emergency exit played an important role in the fact that some survived the massacre as it was through this door that many were able to escape.

Reflections

January 10, 2016

Last Sunday, our neighborhood was once again the site of a national event.[1]
A national homage to the victims of the attacks was organized on the
Place de la République, in the presence of the French President, François
Hollande, and the Mayor of Paris, Anne Hildago. Along the Boulevard
Voltaire the cars were replaced by pedestrians moving toward the Place de
la République.

---

1   On that day, January 10, a "Memory Oak" was planted on the western side of the
    square (see map and discussion in the Introduction and Conclusion). A plaque
    was also laid at the foot of the tree, with the inscription: "In memory of the vic-
    tims of the terrorist attacks in January and November 2015 in Paris, Montrouge
    and Sain-Denis. The French people pay homage to them here".

I wonder if the square would have had the same destiny in the wake of January 2015 if it hadn't been renovated in 2013 to make it a pedestrian zone? If the square had remained in its previous form, with cars and buses crossing from all directions, the meeting place would possibly have been the Place de la Bastille — a traditional site for major demonstrations and civic meetings. The Charlie Hebdo office on Rue Nicolas Appert is closer to Bastille than to République (1 km compared to 1.2 km). All around France, urban planning policy and memory policy are intricately connected. In this particular case, municipal decisions on urbanism have influenced the form that both the official and spontaneous commemorations have taken.

From my perspective as a local resident, it was clear that this ceremony was not very successful. The crowd was small, and the residents of the neighborhood made their indifference clear. Some of them seemed to be waiting for the visitors to leave, so that they might go back and explore their "domain". I took an intermediary stance; as a resident I was in the background, but as a sociologist I was anxious to see for myself, so I attended the last part of the ceremony.

More specifically, I attended part of the ceremony from one section of the square. Indeed, this ceremony was set up as a *mise en abyme*, as a kind of game of mirrors, of reflections. A spatial distinction was created in the square, reflecting the former division of the space in two for the cars to circulate. The "real" ceremony, in the presence of François Hollande, was performed on the side of the 10th arrondissement, while the other side of the square (the 11th arrondissement side) was reserved for onlookers. We were able to watch the event through its re-transmission on a giant screen, which reflected everything that was happening on the "other side" while also functioning as a kind of barrier.

But this mirror was also temporal. Once the ceremony had finished, the screen continued to replay the images. These images were not of the past being commemorated, nor of lessons to be learned from it, but of the commemorations themselves. Standing in front of the statue of Marianne, we thus saw replay images, reflections, of the statue of Marianne taken at different times since January 2015. These reflections within reflections limited the horizon of the commemoration itself by establishing it in a cyclical mode rather than a linear one.

This approach to commemoration is not new. Among the many national commemorative days set up by the French state since the year 2000, two dates have been chosen in this particular mode, due to lack of consensus and political will about the meaning, or the "message," to give to the commemoration in question. For example, in 2003, December 5 became a national day of homage for those who died for France during the Algerian war and the battles in Morocco and Tunisia.[2] Yet rather than commemorating a specific event in this war, the date was chosen as a reference to the inauguration of a monument to honor these soldiers by the President of the Republic, on December 5, 2002. Similarly, since 2006, May 10 has been considered the national day for remembrance of the slave trade, slavery, and their abolition; but the choice of the date primarily refers to the Senate's unanimous passing of the law recognizing slavery and the slave trade as crimes against humanity (Gensburger, 2014).

In these two cases, the choice of the commemorative date reflects the commemoration itself rather than the event to be commemorated. This stems from the difficulty in delimiting what these pasts were to signify for contemporary society and the lessons that should be taken from them.

2   In 1945, Algeria was an integral part of France. Following the Second World War and the enlisting of many Algerians to fight for the liberation of France, demands for independence and autonomy began to emerge. They were initially repressed by the French state. In 1954 the war broke out and went through several phases until independence was finally won on July 3, 1962. A ceasefire had been signed by both parties on March 19, 1962, but it was followed by further killings of Harkis (Muslim Algerians who had served France) and Europeans who remained in Algeria. This is why certain memory actors refuse to consider March 19 as the date of the end of the war. Similarly, between 1952 and 1956, conflict broke out in Morocco, a French protectorate, which became independent on March 2, 1956. After a broadly comparable process, independence and the end of its status as a French protectorate, were also proclaimed for Tunisia on March 20, 1956.

Messages

January 11, 2016

On Monday morning, the day after the national commemoration, new messages appeared along Boulevard Richard Lenoir. New images, new clichés are now studded along the railings.

Laminated images of messages taped to the fence, are themselves taped to the railings in turn. Pictures of candles hang above real candles. The choice of black and white, symbols of the past, add to this commemorative reflection. Like yesterday on the Place de la République, the self-reflexive gaze of the commemoration is once again reflected here.

Of course, other new messages speak of the Republic, "solidarity," and of "living together." There is also a small but very explicit minority which projects a virulent critique of Islam.

In between these two extremes there is a general tone of patriotism.

Around noon, in front of the Bataclan Café, just as the rain is forcing people to seek shelter under the awning, a man walks by and gives the Nazi salute to the small crowd. His gesture is accompanied by a loud "Heil," which leaves no room for ambiguity.

Behind the self-reflexivity of the commemoration, the messages that are expressed are extremely diverse, sometimes irreconcilably so, in diametric opposition to the consensus sought by the commemorative event itself.

Detour

January 12, 2016

In France, and particularly in Paris, this *mise en abyme* of the commemoration which has characterized recent days is not new. It was born with the Republic.

Founded under the July Monarchy,[1] in 1837, the Museum of the History of France within the Château de Versailles, was designed to commemorate the nation's past through the commissioning of artwork. My colleague, Sylvain Antichan, has meticulously and vigorously studied the ways in which the state, through this museum, has depicted France's history through paintings. Up until the Third Republic, the themes celebrated here include important battles and their heroes, coronations and kings (Antichan, 2014).

However, after the establishment of the Republican regime in 1870, more and more paintings concerned not so much the events or the men involved, but rather the ways in which these events were celebrated. Under the Third Republic, representing a ceremony that pays homage to the past became one of the most common ways to evoke national history. In one painting, for example, which hangs in the Museum of the History of France,

---

1   In 1830, Louis-Philippe of the House of Orleans, ascended to the throne of France. He lost the throne in 1848 with the establishment of the Second Republic, which lasted only 4 years before the Bonaparte's *coup d'état* and his coronation as Emperor.

Marshall Foch is not portrayed through his military actions, but through the homage paid to him at the Arc de Triomphe.[2]

This detour through the past (and through Versailles, and the 8th arrondissement where the Arc de Triomphe stands) allows us to put the commemoration of the January 2015 attacks into perspective, in light of the long-term history of the Republic. In so doing, it forces us to ask just how novel the contemporary period really is.

2   Gilbert Bellan, Exposition du cercueil du maréchal Foch sous l'arc de Triomphe de l'Etoile, 24 mars 1929, painted in 1929, purchased for Versailles in 1936 and hung in the Museum of the History of France under the Third Republic (after being hung on the ground floor of the central building) 0,89 x 1,16 m.

Solidarity
January 14, 2016

Turkey was hit by two separate attacks this week. In front of the Bataclan tonight there were — for the moment — no messages that made reference to these attacks. Up until last Tuesday morning there was a message paying homage to the previous attacks in Ankara on October 10, 2015,[1] but it then was collected with the other messages to be conserved by the Paris Archives.

It is out of solidarity, as the text written above the portrait states, that this message was placed here. Solidarity is indeed one of the most frequently reoccurring forms of expression in the sites around the Paris attacks. Identical observations were made after the attacks in New York and Madrid, this post-traumatic cosmopolitanism is striking both for its extent and its limits. Certain messages condemn the fluctuations in this solidarity, making their homages to the victims also a political statement. The railings along the Boulevard Richard Lenoir have thus become a manifestation of the solidarity which, ultimately, connects those who leave these tributes, not so much to the victims of November 2015, as to other groups.

[1]   On October 10, 2015, an attack in Ankara left 102 people dead and more than 500 wounded. A double explosion targeted a pacifist demonstration organized by left-wing forces. This occurred in a context of political tensions in Turkey.

Tourism

January 15, 2016

A new kind of visitor has appeared in the 11th arrondissement. Often with a map of Paris in hand, tourists — for that is who they are — have become a familiar sight in the "Bataclan neighborhood." Local residents often see them as intruders, drawn here by the blood and tears. Indeed, it is not unusual that these visitors take photos — selfies even — of the bullet holes in the walls around the concert hall.[1]

This macabre attraction, known as "dark tourism," has given rise to numerous studies on wide ranging subjects — from the camp at Auschwitz, to New Orleans after Katrina (Miles, 2002; Hernandez, 2008; Lisle, 2004). This approach is undoubtedly useful in providing meaning to some of the visits to number 50 Boulevard Voltaire. It is not sufficient, however, to understand this new kind of tourism as a whole.

In 2000, Rachel Hugues, an Australian geographer, began to study visitors to the *Tuol Sleng Museum of Genocide Crime* in Phnom Penh, which, at the time, literally displayed the tortures and crimes of Pol Pot's regime in Cambodia (Hughes, 2008). Her conclusions led her to nuance the motivations for dark tourism. She observed that ultimately the visitors were not very interested in what they saw; they did not go to these sites to satisfy a supposed fascination for evil, but rather to respond to a social injunction for compassion. From this perspective, the influx of tourists to the area around the Bataclan may not be a sign of sordid moral deviance, but on the contrary, a form of moral conformity to humanism.

Although it does nothing to relieve the feeling of intrusion for many residents, such a hypothesis encourages us to look at this new kind of visitors in a different way.

---

1 See "Photography", January 9, 2016.

▲ A tourist holding a map, photograph taken yesterday, January 15, at 5.40pm on Boulevard Richard Lenoir across the road from the Bataclan.

Nationality
January 17, 2016

Both on the Place de la République and in front of the Bataclan there are still many flags, even today. French flags of course, but also the flags of other countries. Should we consider these flags as "foreign?" They are of course; France has only one flag. But perhaps they are more than that.

These flags are sometimes left by tourists, but the chronology suggests that they are also put there by Parisians, either of French nationality or not. Just after November 13, several texts — now preserved in the Paris Archives — expressed the solidary of particular groups of Parisian residents — Haitian, Sri-Lankan, Portuguese, Iranian or Kabyle. How should we interpret this expression of a particular group's solidarity with a national cause?

For some, these signs suggest that these populations feel French. For others, they are yet another sign of the fragmentation of French society. In France, commentators regularly present "patriotism" and "communitarianism" as in opposition to each other — identifying patriotism with the ideal of unity and indivisibility of the Republic. The reaction to the attacks encourages us to move beyond this dichotomy, however, and to re-think these "codes of difference" as Riva Kastoryano has called them (2008). The blossoming of these flags in fact supports the hypothesis that individuals can feel like they belong to several nationalities at once — feeling both as though they are from here and elsewhere, or even feeling like they belong here *because* they are from somewhere else, and vice versa.

Indeed, it was in the wake of the January 2015 attacks that I realized how many people in the 11th arrondissement, and in Paris more widely, had connections with Kabylia.[1] Since the gathering on the Place de la République on the evening of January 7,[2] I had noticed the presence of several Kabyle flags. On January 11, during the enormous demonstration that followed the attacks,[3] I was again struck by the number of these blue and yellow flags among the crowds that had invaded the neighborhood. In the research that will inevitably be conducted on the reactions to the "Paris attacks" — because that is how they are now known — it is important to pay attention to the ways in which different forms of belonging have been expressed, including in mutual reinforcement.

1   Kabylia is a northen region of Algeria whose people have been claiming autonomy first from the French state and, after 1962, from the Algerian one.

2   Parisians spontaneously gathered together on the Place de la République, immediately after the killings at the Charlie Hebdo offices and on the Boulevard Richard Lenoir.

3   On January 11, 2015, 2 million people demonstrated in Paris, in protest against the attacks that had occurred the week before. Several commentators described this march as "republican".

Nation

January 18, 2016

Today I am not in Paris, but in Grenoble, a provincial town at the foot of the Alps. The center of town here bears almost no traces of the November attacks. Only a banner with the words "Je suis Charlie"[1] hanging on the façade of the local regional newspaper office is a reminder that, in 2015, France was the target of a wave of attacks.

Here there are, of course, no crime scenes at which to pay homage.

Nor are there French flags in shop windows, or instructions on where to seek psychological support. The residents here have a completely different normality to those who live around the "Bataclan neighborhood."

This is by no means a criticism. Just an invitation to think about what constitutes the "national" nature of an event and what links people together when they live in the same territory.

But what territory is that really? A country? A town? A neighborhood? A street?

The lack of traces left by these events in the urban space here is not, of course, a sign of indifference and — conversely — their omnipresence in

---

1   In the wake of January 7, 2015, the slogan "Je suis Charlie" (I am Charlie) went viral on social networks as well as in demonstrations and on posters in the public space. It became a symbol through which to manifest one's concern and solidarity with victims. It also had other forms, such as "je suis hypercasher" (in reference to the Jewish supermarket that was attacked, see Conclusion), or "je suis français"...

Paris and my own neighborhood must not by systematically interpreted as empathy. Other dynamics, for example social conformity, may play a role. Several provincial schools, as well as schools overseas, in fact sent letters and drawings to my children's school as a sign of solidarity, both after January and November 2015.

The fact remains that this experience of being removed from my everyday life within the "Bataclan neighborhood" — of being de-centered — has been deeply unsettling for me.

How is the nation built as a community of experiences? Even as calls are made for national unity, can we in fact talk about these attacks as a single, unified, national experience?

Normality

January 21, 2016

Understanding people's behavior in society is one of sociology's main reasons for existing. As Bernard Lahire reminds us in a recent book, sociologists do not look for "excuses" for individuals, first and foremost because their research questions are never framed in normative terms (2016).[1] This does not mean that sociologists are never moved, horrified or traumatized. Of course they are, just like any other individual. And on November 13, they were. And many of them — including myself — will remain traumatized for a long time to come.

Simply put, a sociologist's questioning of the world is the result of an active process of distancing oneself; a form of emancipation — always imperfect — from one's emotions and convictions. Emile Durkheim, the founding father of French sociology, used the evocative term "preconceptions" to refer to these ideas which exist prior to research; these ready-made ideas and social assumptions from which the sociologist must break free in order to work correctly. In 1897, Durkheim consecrated his pioneering book to a form of behavior — which was at the time morally condemned — that is not unrelated to the November attacks in Paris: suicide (1897).

Over the last few weeks, the media description of the perpetrators of the November massacres has evolved significantly. The attackers were not drugged after all. We must face the facts: at the time of the events they were

---

1   The term "excuse" is a reference to comments made by the Prime Minister Manuel Valls, on January 10, 2015, following the attacks: "For those enemies who attack their fellow citizens, who tear up the very contract that binds us together, there can be no explanation. Because to explain such actions would be, in a certain sense, to excuse them."

▲ Photographs taken January 9 on the fence of Boulevard Richard Lenoir, around noon.

in their "normal" state, they were fully aware of what they were doing. Studies have already been conducted on how someone becomes a jihadist, a process some refer to as "radicalization." More studies will come; And they will undoubtedly focus on the precise moment when theory became action; the moment that led a group of men to murder 130 people during a single night in Paris.

There are already systematic research studies — from a more historical perspective — on this category of people that Harald Welzer calls *Executioners,* in a book by the same name. His book's subtitle is evocative: *From normal men to mass murderers* (2008). Welzer studies the ways in which German soldiers, who were not fervent Nazis, progressively accepted to execute Jews, including children, at close range, and he challenges our commonplace perception. His work shows us how to understand, but by no means excuse, this action. He suggests that we move away from an analysis in terms of brutalization and toward one in terms of normalization.

If these men were able to morph so easily into executioners, it is not because they were victims of ideological indoctrination, but because they were caught in social groups, peer groups, in which daily interactions made the act of killing perfectly normal. Assassination was a way for them to show solidarity with their brothers in arms and to demonstrate that they were still worthy of their families' trust. In this specific instance, it is ordinary social mechanisms that explain the decision to act: normalization rather than brutalization.

The contemporary situation is undoubtedly different, but the conclusions of this study, and other similar research, such as that by Christopher Browning (1992) or Elissa Maïlander (2015), encourage us to go beyond an approach in terms of radicalization, and to take the "normal" dimension of the criminal behavior of November 13 very seriously.

Indeed, this same normality can be seen today on the sites of the attacks, in spite of the immense suffering that they were (and remain) witness to. It is normal to be shocked, but it is difficult to be surprised. We live in a market-driven society. It is therefore normal that the visitors laying flowers in front of the Bataclan spontaneously led to a rose seller hastily setting up nearby. It is even normal that every time there is a commemoration on the Place de la République, there are people selling French flags to onlookers.

At the fishmonger on the Rue Oberkampf, it is normal that the sign announcing the next sale of oysters, or the brochure on sustainable fishing, is pinned up next to the poster for the psychological assistance available to residents of the 11th arrondissement affected by the events.

The most dramatic events remain social events. This is true for the memories we have of them, which are born of everyday interactions and conversations between the men and women who make up society.

Living in the "Bataclan neighborhood" with two young children makes this normality even more salient for me. Walking by the Boulevard Richard Lenoir, my daughter stopped in front of a doll among the flowers and letters left in homage, closer perhaps to her 7-year-old world than the other tokens. My son, who is only 4 years old, thinks that these flowers and candles are there for decoration. He has made them into a kind of Father Christmas, his Father Christmas, who he says good morning to every day as he goes by.

When the neighborhood is closed off because of an official visit, my son sees the red and white plastic tape set up across the roads as the opportunity to duck underneath and jump over the obstacles, just like his favorite video game hero does. When we pass by candles that have been lit in homage to the victims, he has a normal 4-year old reaction — he wants to blow them out. And I then have a normal motherly reaction, explaining to him that these are candles that people have left there so that they might stay alight — they are not birthday candles.

Data

January 26, 2016

In 1897, Emile Durkheim relied on statistical data to study the causes of suicide. Examining propensity for suicide according to the social characteristics of individuals, he revealed, for example, that marriage was an element that protected men from taking their own lives but made women more likely to do so.

What kind of data can a researcher use to understand what is happening around the sites of these attacks?

As a resident of this neighborhood, I sometimes feel that there are many more visitors since November 2015 and that the people wandering the streets here are not the same as they were before. As a sociologist I am

obliged to question this impression, or at least to put it on hold, until it can be supported by facts, by data.

Yet data does not exist on its own; it must be constructed, and it is never more than one element among the many clues upon which knowledge of contemporary society is based.

As part of its open data policy, the RATP (the Parisian public transport network) also made public the figures on visitation to the different metro stations. Data for 2014 is already online and 2015 will be available soon. Comparing these figures for the months from November to January for each of these years, and for the stations on metro lines 5, 8 and 9 that separate the Place de la République, the Bataclan, and the Charlie Hebdo office, should provide a more concrete perspective.[1]

But once the visitors arrive in the neighborhood, what do they do here?

And who are they?

My spontaneous impression, as a simple passerby, was that these visitors were mainly tourists and that they had come in couples. So, since January 5, either alone or with colleagues,[2] I have conducted several periods of observation with the objective of producing some numeric data and challenging my own impressions as a resident.

---

1   Since this book was first published, this data has been made public. The analysis suggests that the metro usage on the dates of commemoration were not sufficiently large as to alter the standard frequentation figures for the area. There is one exception to this however: immediately after November 13, 2015. During the weekend of November 14 and 15, the frequentation of these metro stations doubled in comparison with the pluri-annual trend, all other things being equal. This data can be consulted here: https://opendata.stif.info/explore/dataset/histo-validations/information/.

2   Sylvain Antichan, Marion Charpenel, Brian Chauvel, Julie Lavielle, Brett Le Saint, Jeanne Teboul and Gérôme Truc.

The first observation is that the profile of the visitors is markedly differ-ent during the week and on weekends and depending on the time of day. However, if we look at the data — which will need to be seen in conjunction with other data, such as that produced by Maëlle Bazin in her work on Place de la République[3] — it seems that tourists are in fact in the minority, even on the weekend. There are almost always more Parisians. Moreover, and to my great surprise, many residents stop, sometimes at length, to see what is new — much as I do, really. On Tuesdays and Fridays, the days when the market is held on the Boulevard, they can be easily identified by their shopping bags and baskets, like in the photo here.

Thus, between one third and half the people who pass by this footpath stop to look, and often to read the messages left here. This observation re-veals the need for in-depth research on the impact that these attacks have had on the neighborhood — much like the study conducted by Gregory Smithsimon on the neighborhood around Ground Zero after September 11 in New York (2012).

Something else that has thrown my impressions into question, is that cou-ples are also in fact relatively rare among the visitors. They had possibly attracted my attention previously because of the gender roles that I had ob-served — indeed there seemed to be a differentiation in their behavior. The women tended to read the texts of the homages more, and in more detail, and to focus on the objects. The men kept their distance, often contenting themselves with an overall vision and often using photography as a media-tor. Thus, within a couple, it was generally the man who took the photos.

The question of gender, which was already central for Durkheim in 1897, seems to be once again an essential element that needs to be taken into ac-count in all the studies that are underway (by researchers or journalists) on what is now described as the "reaction to the attacks."[4]

---

3   Her PhD research, which is currently ongoing, is entitled "Urban writings in the wake of the attacks of January 2015 in France."

4   See the working group that I participate in on the "Social reactions to attacks" coordinated by Gérôme Truc, https://reat.hypotheses.org.

Pilgrimage

February 2, 2016

The term "memorial" is systematically used to describe the statue of Marianne and the objects and texts left on the pedestal. The visitors to the Place de la République thus come to join in the "commemoration," just as François Hollande did last January. Yet the term "memorial" does not really adequately articulate what is happening in this space.

Firstly, a memorial is intended to preserve the memory of something that happened in the past. The repetition of the attacks in November showed that the event which occurred the previous January was neither past nor finished.[1]

Secondly, and more fundamentally, after observing the tributes and homages left and the way in which they have been maintained and preserved, this site appears to be more like a "sanctuary" to which "pilgrims" come, rather than a "memorial." Indeed, many of the texts and objects left mobilize religious symbols in their reactions to the attacks, and this is reflected in the votive candles and in the slogan "Pray for Paris" that circulated on social media at the time.

---

[1]   As stated at the beginning of the book, the chronicles are published here in the same chronological order as they were written. The reader unfortunately cannot ignore the fact that this repetition has by no means stopped since, particularly with the massacre of July 14, 2016 in Nice. The very notion of an event must in this respect be reworked, just like that of an "era" that it now increasingly evokes, see below.

ʌ Photographs taken between January 23 and 29, 2016 around the statue of Marianne, Place de la République. They are just an example among dozens of others that were observed of the tributes which overwhelmingly evoke Christianity (primarily Catholicism but also Orthodox Christianity as well).

Candles are traditional supports for memory in the Jewish religion, as well as part of pilgrimage practices in Catholicism. They are used to heal wounds and banish fears, to protect those who light them. From this perspective, this practice of pilgrimage to the Place de la République embodies and nourishes the fear of the future rather than the cult of the past.

The giant banner with the message *"même pas peur"* — "you don't scare us" — which was originally written with a permanent marker on ordinary fabric, was recently reproduced in professional, weatherproof form. However, this new permanent banner has a meaning that runs counter to the very text that it proclaims;[2] it's reincarnation for posterity is clearly designed to fight against the very fear it declares does not exist. The objects and texts left under the statue are also scrupulously cared for by men and women who have proclaimed themselves the protectors of this space and who behave as though they are the guardians of sanctuaries and holy relics.

In this way, these guardians, who have set up an association under the name "17 Never Again",[3] are clearly marking their territory — which they oversee and care for — just as a religious brotherhood might protect a sanctuary. The creation of a logo and its appearance in several places around the statue and its base are the spatial manifestation of this self-appointed role and the protective appropriation it implies.

In this context, how can we understand the place of the "Memory Oak," planted by the President of the Republic nearly three months ago? This planting seems clearly intended to allow the place of pilgrimage to be moved. Notwithstanding the likelihood that the guardians of the sanctuary do not look favorably on such a move, is such a thing even possible?[4]

2   For a detailed presentation of the evolution of this banner see the chronicle dedicated to it, dated May 22, 2016.

3   Number 17 is a reference to the 17 victims of January 2015.

4   On this point see the chronicle "Return", August 26, 2016.

▲ A member of the group "17 Never Again" (17 plus jamais) at work, on January 29. Two logos of this association are visible in this photograph: one on the giant pencil to the right of the lady and one on a flowerpot on the ground to her right.

Michèle Baussant, an anthropologist of memory and exile, studied the reconstruction of the Catholic sanctuary of Notre-Dame de Santa Cruz (previously in colonial Algeria) in Nimes, a middle size city in the South of France (2002). This move was accompanied by the enormous presence of pilgrims, well beyond the Catholic population alone, and unlike the original site, it included both Jewish and Muslim visitors.

In the case of the Place de la République, and the sites of the attack more broadly, the hybridization of religious references has also been present since the beginning. This can be seen in the syncretism of the candles, but also in many of the texts which mobilize atheism, Orthodoxy, as well as Buddhism, Catholicism, Islam and Judaism.

However, and unlike the case of Notre-Dame de Santa Cruz, none of the relics were moved from the statue of Marianne to the Oak, and access to the statue remained possible after the planting of the Oak (unlike the sanctuary in Algeria, which, after the country's independence in 1962, was lost to the *pieds noirs*, mainly Algerian-born French citizens who then predominantly left for France in a mass exodus).

It is therefore unlikely that the Memory Oak will fulfill its function, with the current state of access and movement of people around the Place de la République.

My Islam speaks of love
My Islam speaks of peace
A wall of solidarity between
Humans means respecting
All humanity, regardless
Of religion or the color of
One's skin, we are all born
In the same way
So mother, let not your
Child become a Kamikaze, let not
Your child destroy humanity
Let us build a wall
Of hope and Peace

▲ Message on the base of the statue. Read on January 29.

Fuck those religious megalomaniacs
I'd prefer an atheist who behaves like a believer
over a believer who behaves like an
Asshole
In "hope of life"
Youssoupha

▲ Message on the railings of the park in front of the Bataclan. Read on January 23.

Property

February 6, 2016

Last Friday I went back to the Place de la République at the same time as the week before (around 5.30pm). When I arrived, I saw an unusual scene — at least compared to what I had seen here so far. A man approached the edges of the statue, not to leave something, but to take something — in this case a chef's hat with the French tricolor on its band. He then went back to his friends who were clearly trying to persuade him to put it back, without success.

Just after the attack, several guitars left outside the Bataclan were also taken by passersby — or should I say "stolen?" Who do they belong to really, these things that are left in homage here?

I don't know if the members of the group "17 Never Again" would describe themselves as the "owners" of the objects left here, commonly described as "tributes." What is certain, however, is that they behave like the owners of the space where the tributes are laid. I found the same woman again who was here one week ago, busying herself around the statue, putting things in order — or rather putting them on show. Each time I have seen her do this, she made choices, and decided to throw away the things that, in her eyes, no longer belonged here. On that night, two full garbage bags would be thrown away.

A municipal street-sweeper was working on the Place during my observation. Seeing the members of the collective "17 Never Again" at work cleaning the statue, he left the rest of the square and joined them, conscientiously sweeping — not the statue itself as the others were doing — but the ground around the base. Each in their own place, in a way.

⌃ Mosaic message of January 5, 2016 "And the Child grew and waxed strong in spirit, filled with wisdom, and the grace of God was upon Him. Love." The biblical quote is from the Gospel according to Luke (2:40), the Child refers to Jesus. The word love was added in English in the original message.

Although the same woman I saw a week ago was once again present, there were several new changes that have appeared since the last chronicle. The "Memory Oak" seemed to have been incorporated into the 'property' of the group, who were now taking care of it too. It is now also part of the staging of memory. There was a flowerpot in the center with the logo of the group on it.

The "Memory Oak" is in the process of becoming a derivative of the main memorial.

Yet, last Friday, there was something here that was absent from the base of the statue of Marianne. Little blue mosaic tiles of blue and yellow formed a phrase around the base of the tree. It was written "Love one another," from the Gospel according to Saint John (13:34). Today they are still there, but they have been moved around to make a new message, which still has a biblical dimension.

Invisibility
February 8, 2016

The third of the images reproduced on the next page was taken on the Boulevard Richard Lenoir, in front of the plaque erected to honor Ahmed Merabet, on Saturday January 16, some 10 days after the graffiti message *Je suis Ahmed*[1] (I am Ahmed) was written on the pavement in the colors of the French flag. Today the graffiti is completely washed away.

It is now invisible, but has it completely disappeared?

Across the road from this plaque there is a vacant lot that is destined to become a long-awaited park for the 11th arrondissement, which doesn't have many green spaces. This urbanism project has been underway for several years. Now it is tied up in discussions about whether a memorial should be constructed to the victims of January and November 2015 in the neighborhood, in what form, and where. I don't know if these questions are being asked at the level of the Paris City Council, but they are conversations that arise regularly among residents of this neighborhood when we speak of this future garden.

An Anglo-Saxon friend of mine, who lived in the United Kingdom for a long time, says that — as is customary in London — the garden should be named after one of the victims, Ahmed Merabet, who was killed just across the road, and whose life seems to her to be a particularly good example for younger generations.

---

1   This expression is of course adapted from the iconic one "Je suis Charlie" (I am Charlie).

∧ The message washing
away. Photographs taken
between January 6 and
February 3 2016.

Other residents fear that if a monument were erected it would take up too much space — both physical and symbolic — even though they also hope that such a monument might channel all the other homages in the neighborhood into a single place.

Examples taken from Antiquity as well as from the contemporary period may serve to shed light on this debate. They show that a memorial can also be invisible, and that it is often in this case that it has the most effect.

At the beginning of the 1990s, a German artist, Jochen Gerz, secretly — with the help of students in the Arts College — turned over 2146 cobblestones on the square in front of the Sarrebrück Castle, which was the headquarters of the Gestapo during the war and then the seat of the regional parliament. The number 2146 corresponds to the number of Jewish cemeteries in Germany. The undersides of the stones were engraved with the names of these cemeteries. The invisible monument was born.

Paul Veyne is a historian of Antiquity and he has published several articles on the example of the Trajan Column, a very visible monument in Rome. However, this column commemorates the victories of the Empire so high up that they are inaccessible to people, and thus remain completely invisible to roman citizens, both in Ancient Rome and today (Veyne, 2002). He shows that this invisibility is not by any means a weakness, but on the contrary is a sign of the efficacy of the column as a commemorative monument — expressing simply something that occurred and, in doing so, reaffirming in this very fact, the power of the Roman Empire. He talks of the pragmatic strength of the monument, by opposition with its semiotic strength — the monument *is* more than it *says*.

In both these examples, the effect on passersby is intensified by invisibility. It operates not in terms of the transmission of a narrative of the past, nor of its lessons, but as the social manifestation of the importance of this past, even if it is liable to mean different things for different people.

Witnesses

February 13, 2016

For a long time, I hesitated in choosing the title of this post.

"Witnesses" or "residents?" "Witnesses" *because* "residents?"

Indeed, over the last few weeks, the number of projects collecting the testimonies of those who live here has increased remarkably. This is not simply a matter of wandering around the neighborhood talking with people and trying to understand what they experienced, but a desire to make them talk, to film them, to record them, in order to keep a record of what those who were "touched" by these events lived through — in the words of one of these initiatives.[1]

It is undeniable that the whole neighborhood was touched by the attacks.

Shops here have seen their custom and profits decrease.

Many inhabitants are still anxious, struggling with what they saw that Friday night, and what they continue to see every day — from the bullet holes in the walls, to the piles of tributes, and the endless visitors.

The children who live here have had — and some still have — nightmares, hallucinations and panic attacks. Their parents, including myself, shudder at every siren that lasts more than two seconds, and we all take a step back when we see blue lights flashing in the distance at the Place de la

---

1   The two main ones are "Every witness counts", a data collection program run by the Institute for Present History (*Institut d'Histoire du temps present*) and Radio France, and the "November 13" program run by the National Center for Scientific Research (CNRS) and Inserm, in collaboration with the National Audiovisual Institute (INA).

République — even though it always later turns out to be the police pre-venting an illegal gathering or overseeing a demonstration.

When I began these chronicles, I chose to not make them a personal diary, or a diary of any kind. Not out of principle, in fact as part of these writings I have had to take a lot of notes on my/our everyday life, but simply because that is not my style of writing. Another mother in my children's school, a journalist, has done it in her own way too.[2]

But on a more personal level, it is clear that life has returned to "normal" around Boulevard Voltaire, even though the attacks are "still there." It is thus in the heart of the most ordinary experiences that the events of November 13 reemerge. Last Saturday, this happened during an ordinary conversation with two mothers of my daughter's friends, at a birthday par-ty she was attending. We were talking about the cake when all of a sudden one of them asked "And where were you on the night of the attacks? And the children?" Then there were tears and a traumatic story about the expe-rience of a big sister of one of my daughter's friends.

However, there are many ways of recounting the peculiar state in which our neighborhood finds itself, and it is not sure that compiling several hundreds, or even thousands (depending on the project) of "testimonies" — especially prioritizing those with image and sound — are the most appro-priate way to grasp in depth just how this event has marked the "Bataclan neighborhood" and its residents, in all their diversity.

Do the residents want to talk?

There are psychological support and group therapy sessions provided by the municipal Council, and they are attended of course, but only by a rel-atively small number given the population affected. Residents also feel the need, if not to turn the page completely, then at least to be able to not have it constantly open. I have also been present at several disputes among friends and parents on this question, some demanding that the subject be dropped.

2   See www.lesjours.fr and the chronicle "Journalists" du 7 mars 2016.

Other observers talk about repressing memories, and perhaps that is true, but freedom today is also the freedom to repress. It is therefore not certain that the arrival of teams of researchers/ directors, *en masse*, will be met with open arms.

And who are these residents anyway? Who must stand "witness?"

These large-scale projects compiling oral archives — because that is what they are — are clearly inspired by the studies long conducted worldwide among the survivors of the Holocaust.

Even in that case, despite the fact that the extermination itself had given rise to categorizations, determining who was concerned was no easy matter, but here?

Of course, those designing these studies, some of who are colleagues, are conscious of this and will undoubtedly be methodical in their approach. The studies which were conducted in New York after September 11 will also serve as a model.[3]

Yet these events are very different, and the urban fabric of the two cities even more so. In the case of New York, the question of who was to definitively become the spokespeople for history was not unproblematic. In the contemporary projects in Paris, it may be reasonably feared that only those "witnesses" who know how, who are able and who are willing to speak will be immortalized on film.

On January 9, my colleague, Brian Chauvel agreed to spend some of his time with me, observing the areas around the Bataclan. While there, he met a man wearing a yellow baseball cap, carrying two large bags, one a plastic supermarket bag. He was from Mali and he talked to Brian informally, in broken French. He was used to walking this way, he said; he had come to look for the photograph of a man who volunteered in distributing free food

---

3   See the 9/11/2001, Oral History Project at Columbia University in New York (Bertin-Mahieu, 2017).

"for the hungry" at République, and who had always been very nice to him.[4] He had not seen the man since November 13 and had been told that he had been killed in the Bataclan. He didn't know his name and had wanted to come and pay his respects to him.

For several months, well before the attacks, this man passed along the Boulevard every day to go to the place where hot lunches were served in another part of the neighborhood. Now, every time he passes, he looks to see if the man's photograph has been added. He was very upset when he talked about it, just as he was when he described his own experiences of the night of November 13, a night without sleep, talking endlessly with his fellows on the street.

Because yes, this "witness" lives on the street. Yet he is no less a resident of the neighborhood and was clearly "touched" by the events. It is highly unlikely, however, that his experiences will be preserved among the testimonies currently being collected.

If, as our political representatives tell us daily, these attacks in January and in November are only the beginning of a long series of attacks,[5] will we record hundreds of thousands of "testimonies" among the "residents," every single time?

There is a form of fetishism in wanting to capture and preserve the words of these "witnesses" (along with those of the "victims," injured or near death) as though it could prevent the repetition of these events.

Today, I cannot give a face to one of these witnesses rather than another, even from behind.

Today no picture would be enough.

---

4   The Place de la République has been a site for the distribution of free meals for a long time.

5   Once again, the period between the writing of this chronical and the publication of the book has unfortunately confirmed this fear.

Collecting Messages

February 16, 2016

At the Paris Archives, in several regional archives in different areas of France, in neighborhood collectives, as well as at Harvard University, conservationists, archival staff and citizens have been involved (sometimes since January 2015) in collecting, cleaning, conserving and sometimes digitalizing the texts, objects, drawings, and graffiti provoked by the attacks. The media have already freely reproduced some of these documents, focusing on the more graphic, while others have become almost invisible. Artists have photographed them and now exhibit their work. Publishing houses want to compile these documents into books. Finally, researchers, myself among them, are impatient to be able to closely examine the traces that have been archived, and to try and give meaning to them. These mobilizations are without any doubt important and clearly understandable.

However, living in the neighborhood where these homages are left, and seeing them every day makes one acutely aware of the precautions that must be taken in interpreting them.

Firstly, it is clear that the homages left in the public space and open air are fragile, subject to theft[1] as well as to the elements. To the great disappointment of the man from the commemorative organization "17 Never Again," who collected the texts to laminate and who I met again at the Place de la République on the 30th of December,[2] not everyone thinks to laminate their letters or drawings before leaving them in homage. The wind and the rain are often the first to influence the messages that remain. We could

1   For an example of this, see the chronicle "Property", of February 6, 2016.
2   See the chronicle "Traces", January 30, 2016.

hypothesize that not everyone thinks to, or is able to, protect their messages before leaving them, and that those that do so are possibly more likely to be leaving specific kinds of artifacts or texts, which they intend to last. The more fragile messages, by those who do not plan for posterity, will ultimately become invisible for history.

▲ Boulevard Richard Lenoir, across the road from the Bataclan, a spray painted board that brings together messages with different content to create a new composite document. In this photography, it has been knocked over by the rain and the wind, on February 9, 2016. The other side of this board is in the next picture.

Protecting one's message from the whims of the weather implies that one feels perfectly legitimate in publicly expressing one's thoughts and feelings, and suggests a delimitation between those that do so and those that don't: do women think to protect their messages more than men? Vice versa? Do tourists do it more than Parisians? Or is it more those who have a higher level of education and good French language skills? Or the opposite? So many other questions are raised, perhaps poorly framed, but which remain without answers.

Gathering for escapees from the Bataclan and the cafés

Objective:
to bring together all those who escaped
the attacks, and their loved ones,
in order to express feelings, share
and communicate ideas,
so that this can't happen again.

FB:
Gathering for escapees
from the Bataclan and the cafés

I am
OUAGADOUGOU !
With all my heart

IN TERNATIONAL
DE JUSTICE
VOUS COND...
A ÊT
TIVE
GOM
MÉMOIRE DES
HOMMES l
EXÉCUTION
IMMÉDIATE.

^ Individual messages stuck onto the painting in their order of appearance. I noted the dates
at which I observed them first, respectively December 28, 2015, January 19 (the attack on
Ouagadougou occurred on January 15)[1], January 20, and January 31, 2016. Transcription
of the texts in the images by order of appearance.

1   On the evening of January 15, 2016, a bar, a restaurant and a hotel in Ouagadougou,
     the capital of Burkina Faso, all primarily frequented by foreigners, were attacked by
     members of Al-Qaeda in the Islamic Maghreb.

Hope

I watch with patience
Your parade, in my obstinacy
I observe without moving forward, to judgment
Only by curiosity pushed
Terrified, you run circles
Blinded, you believe in your demons
In the void, your actions are made without foundation
It is anger and fear that make you terrifying
I see you scream
I see you cry
I see what too easily invades you
Peaceful in the face of your cries, time will tell
Yet sometimes it happens
That in the darkness, I drown
But I'm much too strong
I carry you in the depths of yourself
And when finally you understand
I appear without adornment
In all my simplicity
To invade your wounded minds.
Chasing their fear, leaving the laughter
This time, in the quest to heal you
Exploring your vibrant souls
Scattering your shining tears
Hidden until your call
Angered by your violent quarrels
I am joy, I am love
I am your voices, illuminating your daring
Your courage on earth helps me see
I am life! I am hope!
Chloé
So many hugs and kisses and
Support from Montpellier
Just NEVER let this happen again!!!!!!
Anyway, we're not afraid
Audran

▲ The sign on February 8, 2016, covered in five texts by different authors.

Finally, the place where the messages are laid develops a kind of auto-nomous existence and in turn structures the reactions to the attacks that will be conserved for posterity. I don't know when this wooden sign initial-ly painted with the just word "love" was left. The first trace I have of it is from December 20, 2015. The sign was empty of any additional texts then, but other people progressively added their messages to it, laminated and glued onto the wood.

It is clear that these homages can, and should, be analyzed separately, and they will be. Yet they now also form a whole, it has become impossible to separate them. So how can we conceive of the collective author of this new ensemble?

Groups

February 24, 2016

People often visit the Bataclan, alone, in families, or accompanied by groups of friends. I still regularly encounter group visits — although less often than before. As I returned home from a family walk, on Sunday January 31, I observed a group of a dozen teenagers, along with three adults who had arrived on bikes. I haven't been able to understand what brought them there.

On January 28, Danièle, a friend and neighbor of mine, took this photo-graph of a group of Egyptian students, who had come to visit the Bataclan. This is the photo that inspired this chronicle; the image is striking both by the size of the group, made up of boys and girls, but also by the staging.

They stand here, flags in hand, posing for the photographer — one of their friends is standing next to Danièle to take the photo. Why such a picture?

The white flag in the lower left-hand corner contains a logo that enabled me to identify the standard of a University in Cairo, a scientific and international institution. I decided to hide the faces of the participants, most of them young, as students are. I made this decision because I found no trace of this photograph on the internet, and thus no record of its public use. I looked on the University website and Facebook page, I conducted a reverse search using Google images and Tineye, without success. Not wanting to misread the meaning that these students had intended to give the photo nor their intentions for its use (a simple private souvenir of a shared moment, perhaps, albeit in a public space), I decided to protect the anonymity of the group.

The question remains, however.

Why such a visit? The faces are smiling and the image conveys a genuine joy of being together — here in front of the Bataclan Café.

With the students waving the flags of their country and their school, the scene has all the characteristics of a manifesto — but of what?

Holidays
February 28, 2016

In Paris children are on winter break, so I haven't been walking past the Bataclan every day on the way to school. But I have returned on three occasions, for roughly forty minutes each time. To observe.

The intersection of Boulevard Voltaire and Boulevard Richard Lenoir has recently been transformed, both in its appearance and in those who visit it.

The tributes and flowers that occupied a large part of the Boulevard Richard Lenoir have practically all disappeared. The reader can compare the photo of the empty green railings, with other previous photos of the same space, laden with flowers and messages.

The crowd barriers are still in front of the Bataclan and also initially remained empty of tributes after the first collection by the Paris Archives. Over the last few days they have begun to fill up again.

The center of attention has once again crossed the road. Today, almost no one visits the side of the park, and the visitors gather again, *en masse*, in front of the Bataclan — in fact in front of the Bataclan Café, next to the concert hall.

These changes did not escape one of my son's friends.

As they walked past, she asked her parents — "are tourists the ones who kill everyone?" A five-year-old's attempt to give meaning to what she sees every day, in connection with something she has never seen but which everyone talks about.

Neighbors

March 1, 2016

Since November, newspaper articles and political speeches have talked about the 'residents' in the areas of the attacks. Future studies will show whether this term was well chosen and whether it is wise to establish a unified group from people whose only shared characteristic is the fact that they live close to where the killings took place.

In any event, the problematic relation between the residents (or at least some of them) and the massacres committed on their doorsteps emerged even before November 13.

Some residents around Charlie Hebdo set up an association as early as Spring of 2015. They preferred the term "neighbors" to that of "residents," calling themselves "Charlie's neighbors."

The objective of these neighbors was to "reclaim their neighborhood and their town, to breathe life and color back into it, to refuse indifference and to feel involved, to demonstrate, with their modest means, that 'living together' is something that can be cultivated, and which needs to be constantly reinvented."

On June 21, some of these residents, including many families, got together to organize a picnic in the Allée Vert which runs across Rue Nicolas Appert, Charlie Hebdo's street. Aiming to counteract the image of sadness associated with their neighborhood, the children and their parents painted the posts that line the Allée with bright primary colors.[1]

---

1   In June 2016, the neighborhood group published a book called *Reprenons notre souffle (Getting our breath back)* by Charlie's Neighbors.

These colors are still there today.

Journalists
March 7, 2016

As the reader knows by now, on January 10, I went to the Place de la République, following the official national ceremony that commemorated the killings in January 2015. Like all Sunday mornings I was accompanied by my four-year-old son. I spent some time observing the square, and then I asked him to wait while I took some "photos of people." He then came up to me and asked quite seriously "Have you changed your job *Maman*? Do you want to be a journalist now?"

This anecdote is a clue to the presence of new figures in our neighborhood: journalists.

It also throws into question my practice of writing these chronicles.

Of course, there were crowds of journalists present on November 14. With their TV production trucks they set up residence on the Place de la République, of course, but also on the central median strip on the road just behind our house. This strip of land, half park, half asphalt is the site of our twice-weekly local market, and a popular playground for local children. Anxious to help our own children settle back into their routine, we were there on Sunday November 15.

This was their first encounter with "the journalists" as my son now calls them. The children's games and laughter disturbed their filming, and their apparent objective to emphasize the "fear in the neighborhood." Our fear was real of course, but it ran alongside other feelings, including the children's pleasure in being together, in running around and laughing.

The presence of journalists declined progressively after this. They returned every time a celebrity came, or a commemoration was held. This photo,

taken on December 8, 2015, when the members of the group The Eagles of Death Metal returned to the Bataclan, is an extreme illustration of this. At the time, I was returning from dropping off my children at school around 9 am, and I didn't know why there were so many black-clothed journalists waiting on the corner of Boulevard Voltaire and Passage Saint-Pierre-Amelot — where there was nothing to see.

Today, the journalists are less visible. Yet since I began writing these chronicles I have thought repeatedly about my son's questions. Am I working as a journalist? I take notes every day about the events and practices I observe, I carefully record words and interactions. I keep records. This is of course all at the heart of what journalists do.

Yet the recent online publication of the newspaper *Les Jours*,[1] has allowed me to become aware of the differences and complementarities between my work, and the work of a journalist who like me, lives minutes away from the Bataclan and who also has a son in the same nursery school as my own. On the website of *Les Jours* she writes a daily blog entitled "November 13: tales from the France that came after." This begins with the personal story of the author, and progressively moves toward interviews with victims or actors involved in the state of emergency.

In these tales, what dominates is the rupture caused by the events. My own chronicles, as conscious as I am of being reflexive and critical, ultimately emphasize continuity. These are two visions of the same reality, written by two different women who both use — at least in part — our different professions to work *with* the events and to try to conceptualize and understand their effects.

1   www.lesjours.fr

Demonstration

March 10, 2016

The messages left on the Place de la République since January 2015 have not yet been exhaustively analyzed — and for good reason. The impression that one gets from this is that there is a call for tolerance and a common agreement to emphasize shared humanity. Of course, this discourse was caused by the violence of the events being commemorated. However, it reflects a tendency that was in place well before the attacks. Several studies have emphasized the way in which collective demands or public policy have presented themselves as being "apolitical" through the register of humanitarianism and human rights (Fassin, 2010).

The nature of the messages left at République, sometimes directly written on the statue itself, have evolved over the last few days. Aside from the accusations of responsibility against political figures, explicit comments not only about France's involvement in Syria or in the Middle Eastern Conflict, previously absent, are now more common. One tag, written in red ink, incriminating the State of Israel, has been scrawled across the pedestal with the dates of the revolution that the statue originally commemorated. The memorial was free from this kind of comment until very recently.

The previously consensual humanitarian discourse has lost ground to more divisive political declarations.

In this respect, and in spite of the monument being protected by the installation of metal barriers (another sign of its official heritage status), yesterday's demonstration against labor law reform has accentuated this conflictual reappropriation of the memorial, although in a completely different register.[1] Several protest messages were added as a result of the

---

1   In March, 2016, the government introduced a bill to reform labor legislation, which immediately gave rise to demonstrations and protest.

demonstration: "Fabius still running,"[2] "power to the people," "Hollande the messenger pigeon and his 40 dictators.... Get out!" "Iraq, Syria. For Oil! Stop the war!". And the trade union flag has replaced the national flags that ordinarily hang on the monument.

▲ "When will true Democracy come?"

Today, the day after the demonstration, this polemical use of the monument, (actually quite diverse in nature) has undergone two changes. When I went past République at 3.15pm I saw a man, with stickers from the demonstration still stuck to his backpack, in the process of folding up the cardboard clown depicting François Hollande that I had photographed the day before. I asked him why he was appropriating the figure and he rapidly explained that he was the one who had made it, and that he'd used his daughter's clown costume to do so. He hadn't been able to reclaim it last night after the march and had come back today, happy and surprised to find it still here. It was in fact at the heart of the memorial, as though strategically placed by the group "17 Never Again," across from Rue du Temple on the south side of the square.

2   Laurent Fabius was then the French Minister for Foreign Affairs.

∧ "Hollande the corruptible. Protect workers' rights".

Since yesterday, the memorial in itself has also been modified, even inside the barriers. The red tag incriminating Israel has been painted over with beige paint (between my visit at 6.30pm yesterday and at 3pm today). Bizarrely however, this message can still be seen, in several different places, on A4 pieces of paper stuck to the pedestal of the monument.

The delimitation of responsibility for the memorial, of its role, and of what it is legitimate to leave there, still clearly remains undefined and is liable to become in itself an object of conflict and contestation.

Paradoxically, the presence of the barriers, which have been in place for several days now, has led to a degradation of the memorial. Probably due to the fact that it has hampered the activities of the members of 17 *Never Again*, the self-appointed guardians of the space. Possibly also because passersby can no longer invest in the space by leaving something, or moving something, or simply by giving meaning and bringing the space to life — even if it is through the register of renewal.

The reappropriation of meaning and finality of commemorative monuments is in fact not new at all. Whether or not this reappropriation is desirable is another question, which goes beyond the limits of these chronicles, but will necessarily be asked by those in charge of the management of public space in Paris.

Conflict

March 17, 2016

Several days before the demonstration against the so-called "El Khomri"[1] law, head-high metal barriers were fixed to the ground around the statue on the Place de la République. Initially I thought that they would be temporary, put there to protect the "memorial."

However, they were still there yesterday. Previous chronicles have described the way in which this protection has paradoxically led to a deterioration of the tributes left at the foot of the statue. Rubbish is no longer collected.

Three days ago, I encountered the woman with the short blond hair who I have seen here on other occasions[2] and who is a member of the association *17 Never Again*. Working with a colleague, she was trying to restore order through the holes in the fence.

Aside from the deterioration of the tributes, these metal barriers and what seems to be their permanent installation, have altered people's attitude to the commemoration. On one hand, there are fewer people who stop to look, or to leave things. On the other, some have adapted, and left candle holders hanging on the fence, or have shifted their attention to the tributes left around the "Memory Oak."

---

1 In reference to the name of the Minister for Labor who put forward this bill in parliament.

2 See "Property" 02/06/2016 and "Pilgrimage" 02/02/2016.

▲ New uses of the metal barriers to hang candles.

▲ New commemorative practices in the other corner of the Place, in front of the "Memory Oak" March 14, 2016.

▲ "Woman, Peace, Freedom" March 16, 2016.

Finally, the presence of the fences seems to be accompanied by the return of a kind of normality to the square. The skaters have reclaimed a large part of the space, and the bikes have also returned. Place de la République has once again become the site of a wide range of political demonstrations which have in turn come to display their messages on the fence, which now forms the barrier between two distinct spaces and restricts memory to a specific area.

Of course, this observation must be put into perspective. Indeed, the situation that I find myself in is common to all researchers in social sciences and extensively theorized. This impression that the space is being reclaimed for uses that existed before the events is in fact likely to also be the product of my own observation.

Today people tend to visit the "memorial" less, and this seems fairly stable. I therefore tend to consecrate less of my time to observing it, and my gaze is drawn elsewhere. Once again this raises a question that is fundamental for any study of social processes in which the observer is both outside and inside the society they observe. This is the issue of knowing whether or not

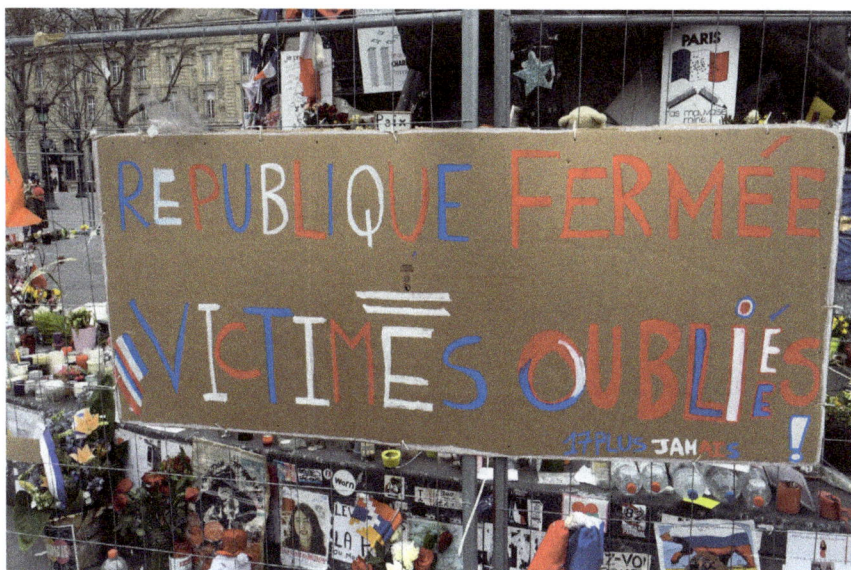

^ "République closed = victims forgotten. 17 never again".

On other cardboard notices like this one, additional comments were written by passersby: "Plaque + tree 50 meters away," "To all our friends in the world who are suffering, from Ivory Coast, Syria and Eritrea. Love and peace on earth" or "If you disagree with the closing of the monument. Express yourself!"

this evolution comes from the social practices of Parisians and tourists, or whether it stems from the (different) way I have been looking at them over the last few days.

For anyone who visits the Place de la République regularly, however, the transformation of the meaning of the memorial is unambiguous. There has been a clear shift from consensus to conflict, which began to appear in the previous chronicle. Yesterday, on March 16, this conflict took on a new form. The group *17 Never Again*, reacted to the 'quarantine' of the monument, which has now been in place for two weeks, by publicly displaying the conflict in ownership around the memorial on one side of the fence, and the public space on the other side. The cardboard posters put up yesterday are also the opportunity for passersby to take a stance in this conflict: "plaque and tree 50 m over there," versus "even death and homage to the dead are regulated"

Since January 2015, we have asked the Paris Municipal Council for a space in which to exhibit and preserve the items (objects, messages, paintings, flags etc.) left by citizens from all over the world, at the Place de la République, in the wake of the attacks.

A petition for this demand will be put forward by the group 17 Never Again, which fights to preserve the memory of all the victims of the attacks.

17 NEVER AGAIN

◄ Transcription of the text on a piece of A4 paper, protected by a plastic sleeve and taped to the barriers in four separate places.

Mobilizations

March 21, 2016

The mobilizations of the members of the group *17 Never Again* seem to have borne fruit. The barriers have been taken down, only a day after they put up the protest posters described in the previous chronicle. On Friday March 18, around 5.40pm, the woman with the short blond hair was back busying herself around the memorial, as she had done before around this time of the week.

The protest posters were carefully put away, face down, around the base of the statue. This weekend they disappeared — put in the bin or archived by a member of the group? A future conflict might tell us.

Now accessible again, the memorial on the Place de la République seems to have entered a new phase. It is now a legitimate space for demonstrations, from those reacting to the attacks, to those in response to the Egyptian revolution, or the fight against the changes to labor laws, as well as those protesting against the policies of the Ethiopian government.

This Thursday was the first anniversary of the attack in the Bardo Museum in Tunisia.[1] Several members of the families of the victims had chosen the Place de la République to pay homage to their dead. They left flowers and photographs. For them, this was also an opportunity to have their voices heard,[2] and to advocate for their cause. This kind of "victims' mobilizations"

---

1   On March 18, 2015, 22 people were executed, and 45 others wounded by members of the Islamic State organization at the Bardo Museum in Tunisia. There were four French citizens among the dead.

2   http://www.lexpress.fr/actualite/societe/attentat-du-bardo-un-an-apres-la-colere-des-rescapes-et-des-proches-de-victimes_1774833.html.

▲ Flowers and photographs of the French victims of the Bardo Museum attack left in the evening of March 17, 2015.

▲ The day after, the same flowers and photographs rearranged by the 17 Never Again.

(Lefranc & Mathieu, 2009) has given rise to several research studies; they appear to be structured by the social relations that existed prior to the event. Trauma alone does not create mobilization, it is also structured by the action of the state.

Here the mobilization for the victims of the Bardo attack was clearly but implicitly guided by public policy. It is indeed by comparisons with the fate — both symbolic and monetary — of the victims of November 13, that the victims of Bardo formulate their demands. It seems consistent therefore to choose the same site to remember "their event," and to situate it in the space of a shared cause with the victims of November and January 2015 in Paris.

The very next day, this mobilization by the victims of the Bardo Museum had been appropriated by the members of the group *17 Never Again*, with a new organization, and the staging of traditional logos such as in the photo below. Here the mobilization has been mobilized.

Other causes have introduced their own organization of the site. On Friday, activists also used the statue and the memorial to draw attention to the cause of the Egyptian revolution.

ᴧ The translation and understanding of this text was made possible with the help of a
neighbor who is a researcher specializing on Ethiopia.

120

Just behind them, a banner, written in Oromo, takes a militant position re-garding Ethiopian politics.[3] It uses the site for homage to the victims of the attacks as a political tribune, proclaiming: "to the memory of the Oromo children massacred in the name of the Master Plan" (a plan to expand the country's capital).

The base of the statue has thus become a place for the conjunction of causes and mobilizations. On Thursday the removal of the barriers had already made room for a large banner — an ode to youth in connection with the demonstration against the "El Khomri" law. This hybridization makes it difficult to create a consensus around a single future site at which to "commemorate the November attacks" and their victims.[4] Proposals for this kind of site continue to emerge. They are in turn the object of further mobilizations.

3   The Oromo people are one of the ethnic groups that make up the population of Ethiopia. In the regions where this group is the majority, its members demon-strated for several weeks against the social and economic inequalities they suf-fer from. These protests were brutally repressed by the regime.

4   In May 2016, the association *Génération Bataclan* made a press release con-cerning the ten proposals for a memorial outside the Bataclan that they had prepared.

Normalization

March 26, 2016

Since Tuesday,[1] certain messages, objects or drawings have been added paying homage to the victims of the recent attacks in Brussels. There are relatively few of them and they have appeared quite progressively.

No gathering took place on the Place de la République in solidarity with the Belgians, even though they are France's immediate neighbors, and they share the same language — or at least some of them do.

The reactions to these new attacks reflect social codes and conventions that are reminiscent of the normalization that occurred around the atrocities of Nazi Germany. Indeed, Harald Welzer described the way in which German soldiers responsible for the extermination progressively learned to kill Jewish people, as following a process of "normalization" rather than "brutalization."[2]

Of course, the killings in Brussels are anything but normal. However there is an impression of the beginning of normalization that has emerged from the observations in our neighborhood this week. Firstly, the management of the memorial has clearly become one of ordinary routine, characteristic of a professional activity. As early as Wednesday night, there was an undeniable expression of solidarity with the Belgian people on the Facebook page of the group *17 Never Again*.

---

1   On Tuesday March 22, 2016, the region around Brussels was hit by three bomb attacks, two inside the airport and another in the subway. These simultaneous attacks killed more than 30 people and left more than 300 wounded.

2   See "Normality", January 21, 2016.

But the images emphasized were primarily the product of a new routine practice of organization, collection, and ultimately fabrication of the tributes in order to give them a coherent message. Thus, on Tuesday 22, at the end of the day, two members of the group were moving around, arranging the artifacts on the base of the statue — artifacts that would be then held up as emblematic the next day on their Facebook page.

I also saw the way in which these events have now taken on a more routine meaning in the (naturally childlike) reaction of my eight-year-old daughter. We walked together across the place on Wednesday evening, and saw a picture of Tintin at the base of the statue, making a direct connection between the Brussels attacks and the Charlie Hebdo cartoonists killed in Paris in January 2015. Aware of what had happened in Belgium, and an avid reader of Tintin, she spontaneously asked me "Oh *Maman*, this time they've killed Hergé?!"

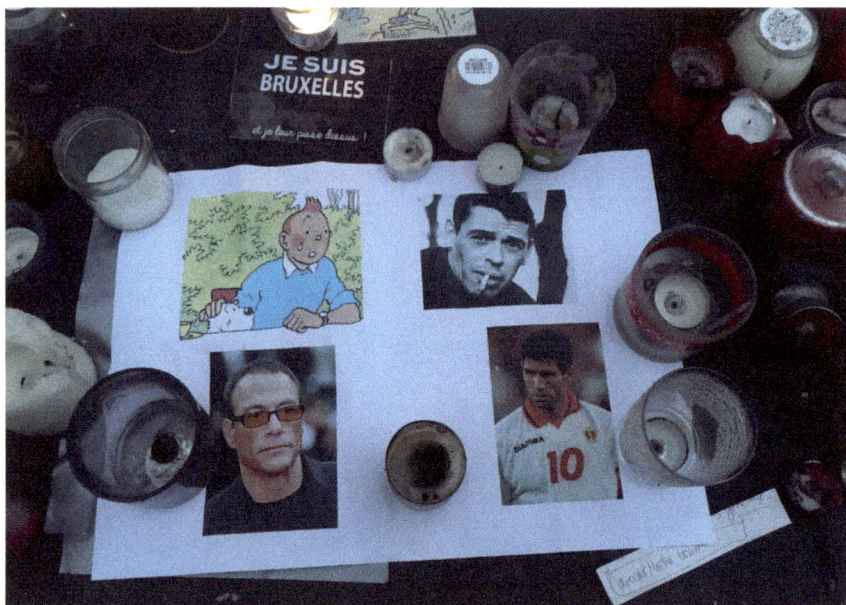

This normalization through practice can be seen in the proposals for monuments and memorials that spring up here and there. For example, the association called *Generation Bataclan*,[3] which is working to have a monument set up in front of the Bataclan, is led by communication professionals who have experience with these kind of issues as part of their jobs.

Similarly, the participative budget recently opened by the Paris Council was seen as an opportunity for several artists to submit proposals for artwork linked to the commemoration of the attacks, also operating from their professional practices.

Finally, it is highly likely that the researchers we have already mentioned, involved in collecting testimonies and working on the social psychology of cohorts linked to the attacks, are already seeing how they can develop the same approach for the case of Brussels, responding once again to professional routines.

3   www.generationbataclan.fr

This normalization currently underway is not only present in the influence of professional trajectories, but also — and this is just one example — in the relationship to place. It is a total coincidence of course, but the day of the attacks in Brussels was also the day that the scaffolding was set up in front of the Bataclan, the first day of the repair work, and the first sign of a return to what everyone in the neighborhood describes as "normality."

This normalization also implies a form of banalization of these spaces, and these events. It is also the indication of a social conviction that it can and will happen again.

It is less like a "return to normal," and more like we are progressively becoming accustomed to living with fear.

Just after the Brussels attacks last Tuesday, the *même pas peur* ("you don't scare us") banner was subject to a further annotation. Someone added — in red pen — the term *"mytho"* (liar). This graffiti shows both that we have moved away from a consensual relationship of respect regarding the memorial, and that at the same time, it is far from being a return to the period before the attacks, because this irreverent message reminds us that the threat is still there.

It was first and foremost this message of threat that echoed around the Place de la République on the night of the attacks in Brussels.

▲ On May 4, 2016, when this photo was taken, the inscription 'Mytho' was still legible.

A Place to Sit

April 8, 2016

The normalization continues on the Place de la République. A week ago, the Place de la République became the hub of the social movement of occupation against the liberalization and the reform of labor laws in France. The movement that called itself *Nuit Debout* (the Night Rises) has been occupying the site each night since then.

▲ Photos taken at different times of the day, between April 4 and 7, 2016.

For the first time since the attacks, people are using the base of the monument to sit on, as they did before January 2015. At night, the participants of *Nuit Debout* sit around the base of the monument. But this return to functionality now also lasts into the daytime. Then it is those who are not participating in the social movements who sit here — to eat, to rest, to wait for someone, or to make a phone call.

This observation raises the question of the articulation between the symbolic and functional dimensions of places and objects, the two not necessarily being contradictory. Functional use can reinforce symbolic range, by naturalizing it.

The fact that the square is now publicly occupied for a reason other than the reaction to the attacks has changed attitudes toward the memorial. These new forms of behavior have led to a reaction by the members of group *17 Never Again*. They frown on these people sitting around the monument, and they tell those who have come for *Nuit Debout* that they should respect the memorial to the victims. In the discussions, they mobilize arguments referring to the pillaging that happened during the COP21,[1] and the impact that that had on the image of the environmentalists. They have put up five copies of their warning message, asking for people to respect the memorial.[2]

1   From November 30 to December 12, 2015, the United Nations Conference on Climate Change was held outside Paris. On November 29, it gave rise to a demonstration by environmentalists and people protesting against the prohibition of demonstrations in the context of the state of emergency. Several participants in this demonstration on the Place de la République damaged and degraded the memorial to the victims of the attacks.

2   The text reads: "Please respect this place dedicated to the victims of the attacks. Citizens are giving their time and energy to clean and preserve the messages, remove the burnt-out candles, put the cut flowers in vases and water the others. Please leave our material here (dustpans, brooms, rubbish bags etc.). This material belongs to us and was paid for by us, we are in no way dependent on the Paris Council. If you would like to borrow something you can ask on our Facebook page, "17 never again", https://www.facebook.com/17plusjamais/ For rubbish, empty bottles and cans, please leave them in the rubbish bins. We are all citizens, let us respect each other. And leave the world clean. Thank you. The members of 17 never again."

Here there are therefore two demonstrations that are facing off against each other and sharing the space of the square: on one side, the group *17 Never Again*, and on the other, *Nuit Debout*.

The second striking change that has occurred on the square is that the multitude of writings is no longer limited to the statue. Although the messages and inscriptions on the statue itself remain for the most part linked to the attacks, the ground of the square is now covered with messages relating to the social demonstrations. Two zones of expression have emerged, and they are very clearly separate. This separation is firstly spatial; there is a kind of limit between the messages relating to the attacks and those relating to the demonstrations. There is a buffer zone between these two spaces that only contains one message with neutral content, compared to the rest of the texts. It bears the sentence "What would we do without us? Resistance and Resilience." The association of the words "Resistance" and "Resilience" is a kind of frontier, a hyphen, between the two spaces on the square.

∧ Frontier space, April 7, 2016

Beware croco-bosses

Rise up and revolt, the system must come down.
Stop exploitation. End the way we live.

Revolution rumbles

Declaration of The Rights of Man Article 35
When a government violates the rights of people – INSURRECTION
is, for the people and for every part of the people, the most sacred
of rights and the most indispensable of responsibilities."[1]

1   This refers to the Declaration included in the June 24, 1793 constitution.

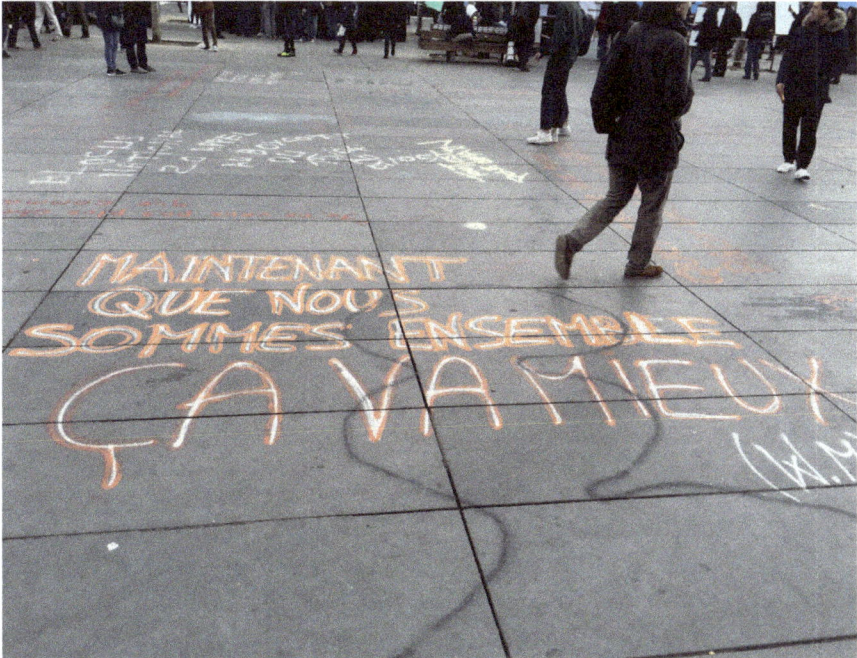

The messages written around the memorial itself are consensual, aiming to bring people together. However, those on the ground on the west side of the square — where the demonstration has set up more permanently — most often express a radical and conflictual opposition between different groups (the state versus the people, the bosses against the workers etc.)

Beyond the spatial separation of the messages, the observation of the space suggests that in the daytime the participants of *Nuit Debout* only very rarely enter the frontier zone and do not look at the memorial. They write their own messages on the square rather than going to read those written at the base of the statue.

Yesterday was April 7 and it was striking to see the coexistence of these two populations, without any contact. On one hand, there were the people mobilized by the social struggle (young adults or retirees, visibly Parisians, sometimes even residents of the neighborhood or from the suburbs around Paris). On the other, there were the visitors to the memorial, who were, for the very great majority, tourists — sometimes with cabin baggage tickets on their bags or with maps of Paris in their hands. This second category also included families from the French provinces, on school holidays, a population mostly made up of middle-aged adults with children and adolescents.

The square is thus a spatial crystallization of a social typology which incarnates a significant divide between different parts of French society. But for an outside observer, there is also the impression that beyond these cleavages, the different causes defended or attitudes, these two populations share the need to come together. As one of the rare non-divisive slogans on the *Nuit Debout* side of the square puts it: "Everything's better now that we're together."

This is an expression that closely echoes the messages of togetherness used by those who came together spontaneously on this square immediately after the attacks in January and again in November.

Reading
April 13, 2016

Place de la République has thus become a place of expression, a forest of messages which becomes a little denser every day. The tributes to the victims of the attacks are now little more than an island in a sea of slogans.

Over the last few weeks the reverse seems to be happening around the Bataclan. The only messages to be seen are those that — not without a degree of irony — announce the security of the worksite during the repair work that has just begun (the blue sign on the café window).

It is thus no longer possible to read the menus from the Bataclan Café, the letter from the Mayor of Paris announcing the collections by the town archives, or the messages left by passersby. This absence of any written

messages creates a distance from the space and implicitly reveals the importance that these words had in capturing the onlooker's gaze, even when what was written was completely disconnected from the events. This includes the plaque explaining the heritage status of the Bataclan building, or the list of dishes available at the café on the evening of November 13.

Everything suggests that this site no longer has anything to say, and thus that in return the visitor no longer has anything to leave here. The barriers put up for the repair work have also led to the few rare tributes being moved — to the side of the café, where it is still possible to see, and read, through the windows. The tributes are thus moved further away from the heart of the attacks — the concert hall being on the right-hand side of the café.

A single message was left recently at the Bataclan — in big red letters. The violence and the crudeness of this message are in contrast to those previously left here. The installation of gray metal barriers seems to have changed the status of the site, and like at the Place de la République, has enabled more polemic messages that were previously very rare here.

This message has since been erased by the town services, although the remains of the red ink are still visible.

It would be interesting to determine the content and the form of what can be written and what should be erased, in the eyes of those responsible for the maintaining public spaces in Paris.

Memories

April 18, 2016

Yesterday was Sunday, and like every day for the last week, the memorial evolved over the course of the day. At 10 am, a trumpet sounded near the statue, a teen band played, boys and girls together. Onlookers gathered to watch the concert. They shared their emotion: "I'm about to cry" said one woman to her neighbor. Playing music in this space, at this time, clearly had a specific meaning for those present. The concert ended with the Marseillaise and the improvised audience sang along. For some, tears flowed for good this time.

The group of teenagers then made their way back to the bus that had dropped them off. One of the adults accompanying them was asked by an onlooker — "That was very beautiful, what you played. Was it for the attacks or for *Nuit Debout?*" The man replied that he had his own "opinions about *Nuit Debout*" but that "it's for the Bataclan, because it's music and they are young people. It's important. We're on the way to a concert and we decided to stop off and play here."

The same place, 8 hours later, and the memorial, and with it the square itself, had changed. The base of the statue was no longer a scene to observe but the space in which the activists involved in the social movement were gathering.

This metamorphosis over the course of the day cannot be summarized by the replacement of a "memorial" cause by another "directed at the future," as some of the messages describe it.

◄ April 17, 2016, the blonde woman from the group 17 Never Again can no longer clean and sweep the pedestal of the statue, because it is now occupied by other people. At a loss, she stands back and watches her co-keeper who is responsible for maintaining the front, and who is trying to set up a makeshift barrier to delimit the space.

Although the members of the group *17 Never Again*, who have looked after the memorial since January 2015, have been progressively excluded from the space, the front of the statue (facing the south side of the square) continues to be maintained and visited as a site for homage to the victims of the attacks.

On one hand, leaving messages and creating traces is a practice that many participants in the social movement continue — from "State of Emergency — my ass!" to "Panama Papers," but also "Democracy where are you?" or "One Utopia, all dystopias," and many others.

Moreover, the traces of the past, these "memories" are also omnipresent in the *Nuit Debout* movement. Yesterday, on the stage of the daily general assembly of *Nuit Debout*, a spokesperson announced a forthcoming demonstration to demand an improvement to services for the victims — not only of November 13 but of all the attacks. More broadly the speakers at the tribune regularly reiterate that the Place de la République is "our space," evoking the demonstrations of solidarity that occurred here immediately after the attacks in January and in November 2015. The past of the square itself is thus implicitly a driving force in the movement.

But the invocation of memory goes beyond the events of 2015. Among the other resources, the past is mobilized to give meaning to the movement. Over the last two weeks, in several different places on the square, different messages have appeared referring to the Paris Commune — the Parisian insurrection of 1871. This reference alone is an important clue as to the origin of part of the demonstrators. In her *Sociologie de la mémoire communiste* (Sociology of Communist Memory), Marie-Claire Lavabre has shown the importance of the Paris Commune in the construction of a communist sense of belonging (1994).

▲ Photography taken April 12 on the East side of the barracks of the Republican guard, Rue Faubourg du Temple. The reference to the Commune is omnipresent on the ground and on the walls of the square.

But the references to the past go beyond the traditional figures of French political history. On Friday night, during the general assembly, the "Migration" Committee of the *"Nuit Debout"* movement was invited to present the results of its research.[1]

The committee's representative raised the question of the *"sans-papiers"* (illegal migrants), but he did so almost exclusively through the prism of the commemoration of the 20 year anniversary of the police evacuation

---

1   *Nuit Debout* was a participative movement that convened daily, at night, in the form of a general assembly. There were also thematic committees such as the Migration Committee, which worked on particular subjects and presented their research to the assembly.

of the Saint Bernard Church.[2] He concluded his speech by proposing that those present participate in the organization of a grand commemoration on August 23. These examples demonstrate the impossibility of separating causes "of the past" from other causes "of the future," or of separating "apolitical" and "politicized" references. Memory is clearly one of the languages of contemporary politics.

A young woman spoke just before the "Migration" Committee, on this same Friday night. After indicating that she had been present on the Place de la République since the beginning, she wanted to make an appeal to recruit willing people to contribute to writing reports for the general assemblies of the movement. This was part of a move to recruit new members for the committee dedicated to what she called "Shared Memory."

2   On June 28, 1996, approximately three hundred foreigners, for the most part unauthorized immigrants, occupied the Saint Bernard Church in the La Chapelle area of Paris. They were protesting against the low levels of regularizations authorized by the new government. On August 23, they were expelled by several hundred policemen who made more than two hundred arrests including women and children.

Place

April 23, 2016

The day before yesterday was the "People's Educational Council" of the *"Nuit Debout"* movement. There was a discussion between the speaker — visibly an academic colleague[1] — and the participants about the concept of heterotopia developed by Michel Foucault. The issue was the defense of the idea that the place de la République is not a place of utopia, but "another place" (hetero-topia), in which it is possible to make, and perhaps to build, something new.

1   Participants in the Popular Education sessions are presented using only their given names.

In response to this proposition, one of the audience members spoke up:

"We are not in another place. We are on this Place de la République, here. It's the same place where other important things have happened; it's the same place as lots of other things."

To this his interlocutor replied, "No, I don't agree. It's the same space but not the same place."

What is Place de la République the "place" of, and how is this inscribed in the space of the square? Does it in fact have a memory? If so, is there room in it for the memories of the attacks and the demonstrations that followed them?

The terms place and space have played a central role in the way that the social sciences have conceptualized memory and the process of memorialization. History as a discipline, and the work of Pierre Nora in particular, has created the expression "lieux de memoire," translated into English as "realms" or "sites" of memory. Sociology, with Maurice Halbwachs, considers memory in its connection to social space, as a structured ensemble of

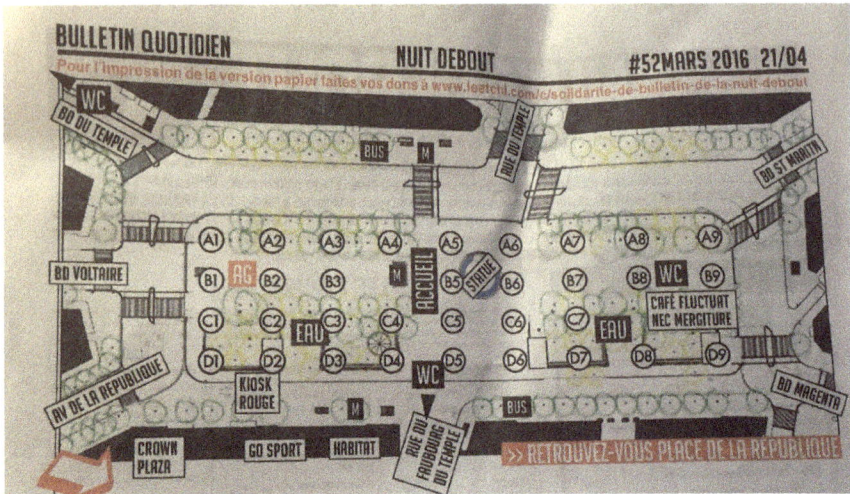

▲ Map published in the daily gazette of Nuit Debout, here on March 52, 2016 (April 21).

relations between individuals. In spite of their profound differences, these two theoretical frameworks create a fundamental connection between space and time. Moreover, for Michel Foucault himself, heterotopias go together with heterochronies (other times). For Foucault, the cemetery, as a place for paying homage to the dead — like a memorial — constitutes one of the best examples of heterotopia/heterochrony (Brossat, 2010).

And the time of *"Nuit Debout"* is indeed 'other.' Their nights are a-social moments *par excellence*; they replace the days and follow each other according to their own calendar, with a single month (March) — of which today is the 54th day. But is it really possible that individuals, who are by definition socialized, can inhabit another space and another time? In this respect it is not insignificant that cemeteries are first and foremost inhabited by the dead.

On Wednesday night, March 51, there was a concert by the *Orchestra Debout*, on the Place de la République. Many commentators and observers described it as a great moment (a "historic" moment) of the mobilization. Several of the reactions and comments that followed emphasized the deep emotion of the participants as they stood before the crowd, which had gathered around such harmony. At several points they referred to the previous

144

emotional high points felt in January, and then in November 2015, in the same place, and within the same space.

That an orchestra could symbolize *"Nuit Debout"* is the sign of the difficulty in creating another place and another time. It is precisely with the example of an orchestra that Maurice Halbwachs explained the way in which collective memory functions, and with it, society. This is taken from his book, *La mémoire collective chez les musiciens* (The Collective Memory of Musicians), published in 1939:

"Let us return to the remark that was our starting point. It was to do with the role of signs in memory, as we have seen in the example of music. In order to learn to play, or to decipher, or even when they only listen, to be able to recognize and distinguish sounds, their values and their intervals, musicians must evoke a certain amount of memories. Where are these memories held, and in what form are they preserved? We said that, if we looked into their heads, we would find a certain number of mechanisms, but which were not established spontaneously. Indeed, it would not be enough for them to appear, to leave the musician alone before these things, to let noises and natural sounds act upon him. In reality, in order to explain these cerebral frameworks, they must be connected to corresponding mechanisms, symmetrical or complementary, which function in other minds, in other people. Moreover, this correspondence could only be accomplished because an agreement had been established between people: but such an agreement supposes the conventional creation of a system of symbols or material signs whose meaning is precisely defined [...] Yet, even the memories that are within the[se people], memories of notes, signs, rules, are found in their heads and in their minds only because they are a part of this society that has enabled them to acquire them; [these memories] have no reason to be other than in relation to the group of musicians, and they are only preserved within them because they are or have been a part of the group. This is why the memories of musicians are preserved in a collective memory which spreads through space and time, as far as their society extends. Yet, in thus emphasizing the role played by signs in musical memory, we must not forget that we could make this kind of observation in many other cases."

▲ Sign carried by a participant of *Nuit Debout*, this text is referring to the collaboration of the French State with the Nazis during the Second World War.

Nuit Debout makes connections between an ensemble of sub-spaces, structured groups, which existed prior to the movement, and which mean that the place is not so much "other" as it is multiple. And this is the reason that even though *Nuit Debout* could be a site for memories (to be expressed), rather than a site of memory. Pierre Nora's acceptance of the "site of memory" is indeed always univocal — it is the historian that gives it meaning. The Place de la République is a space of multiple times, in which everyone gives meaning to the current mobilization, and to past events. Action and memory thus become simultaneously collective.

In this respect, it could be relevant to question the fact that the precedents most often mentioned in reference to *Nuit Debout* — such as the *Indignés* in Madrid, or *Occupy Wall Street* in New York — occurred in towns, and districts that had also previously experienced murderous attacks. But the event of the "attacks" itself only has meaning in a given time and space. In all its "monstrosity," as some commentators have described it, it is read in light of other events, both those that are personal (as we have seen in other chronicles) and those considered "historic," such as the First and the Second World Wars. On the square, in the space of the "memorial" as well as in *Nuit Debout's* space, it is not so much an alternative place and time that are constructed but rather one or several (potentially new) ways of articulating and creating relationships between the times and places that are already there.

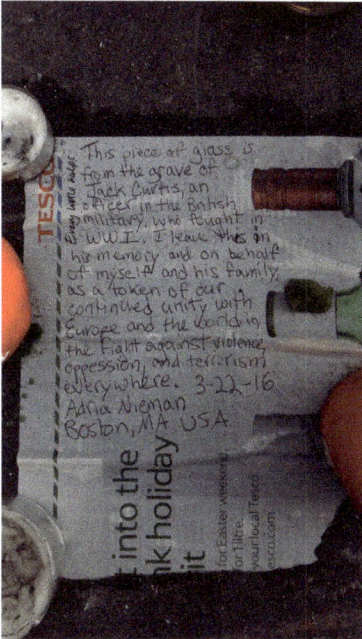

▲ Messages referring to the Second and the First World Wars, laid on the base of the statue in the Place de la République. The first text is in English, the second one is drawing a parallel between the 1930s and the anti-Semitic propaganda and 2015 and the anti-Muslims propaganda "The same mistakes have the same consequences: A World War !!!"

Meaning

May 1, 2016

"*Nuit Debout*" and the attacks share not only space, but also time. Indeed, the killings of November 2015 were also nocturnal. It was at night that Paris was confronted with horror, and it is at night that they now mobilize.

For a regular observer, "*Nuit Debout*" stems in part from a desire to come together, at night, on the Place de la République, in this place and this time that were those of the attacks. Being "debout," literally "standing up," is ultimately a refusal to take it lying down, a refusal to be dead, as so many were on November 13.

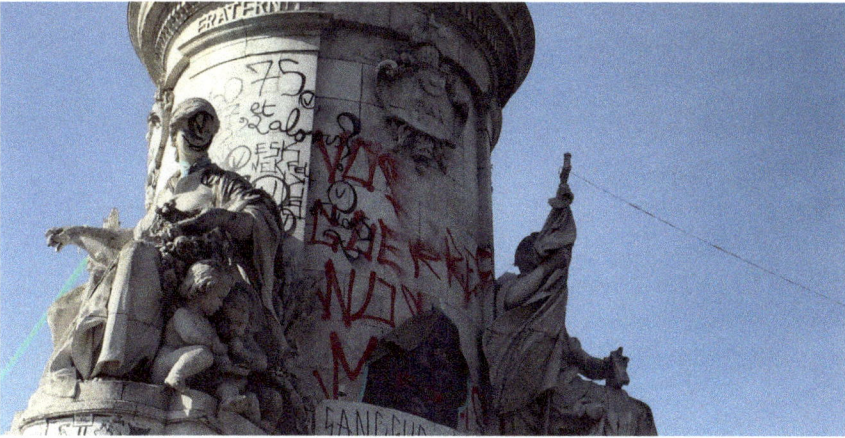

But it also carries a political demand in relation to the attacks. Alongside the demands for social justice, there is also a demand for meaning in the face of this horror — a demand addressed to the political leaders and elites of the country. And this claim is now writ large on the "memorial" statue that towers majestically over the square.

Last night, on the eve of May 1, the ultimate symbolic date of workers' struggles, it was not a message relating to work or finance that was added to the statue. Instead "Your wars, our dead" is now the largest message to appear on the monument. In fact, it is the largest of all the messages on the square.

In this respect, it is not only the count of the "days in March" that characterizes this movement, but also a count of the days since the November attacks. A repertoire of days in an ongoing chaotic period; just as the nights of "*Nuit Debout*" are in themselves, in many ways.

So is it March 62, or November 171?

Post script of May 2

Last night there was another explicit message added, in the same place, "blood on France," "Sang sur la France."[1]

---

1   It had disappeared by May 4.

Seeing and Being Seen

May 13, 2016

Several of the previous chronicles have begun to sketch this — the occupation of the Place de la République by *"Nuit Debout"* reveals some of the deep divisions that structure the memory of the January and November 2015 attacks in Paris.

This opposition can be seen particularly in the attitudes toward the French flag. The base of the statue materializes this disjunction. On one hand the participants in *Nuit Debout* scrawl critical slogans day after day — "an end

150

to borders, burn all the flags" ("*A bas les frontières, brûlez les drapeaux*"). On the other side, on the frontispiece of the statue, on the south side, where the action of the group *17 Never Again* is now limited to, the tricolor dominates.

On face value it thus seems like the two sides of the pedestal correspond to two different political attitudes toward the country — ordinary nationalism and militant internationalism.

Yet, for those who have wandered through the sector between République and Bastille over the last few months, the reality appears more complex, and there are various meanings to be given to the practice of displaying flags.

Since November 13, many Parisians have put up French flags in their windows. On November 25, François Hollande's call to raise the flag in honor of the victims led others to do so too.

▲ Around the Bataclan.

Several commentators have seen this as a form of patriotism, or the display of healthy republican culture. To this day, to my knowledge there is only one study (conducted by Laurent Le Gall and his colleagues at the University of Western Brittany) that has set out to talk to those who, in Brest, put flags in their windows or balconies. The first results of this study are still being interpreted but seem to suggest that the expected explanations do not fit perfectly with the reality. Neither nationalism nor republican culture appear to be the primary motives.

Several hypotheses emerge from this. There seems to be a role for references to other moments of family history in which the flag was brought out, but also quite simply the fact of living in an apartment or a house that is visible, or a street corner that can be seen from far away. Here the physical location of a house has a bearing on whether or not the owner displays the flag.

This is one of the conclusions that the American sociologist Randall Collins arrived at in his study of the "rituals of solidarity" (including flag waving) that followed September 11 in American society (2006). In this case, and in spite of the omnipresence of the star-spangled banner in American society generally, the display of the flag itself specifically concerned primarily urban areas and buildings, because a fundamental prerequisite for the display was that the national colors could be seen from afar. However, Randall Collins' study was primarily conducted in Philadelphia and San Diego, in areas far from the site of the attacks. What about those who lived in the neighborhood itself?

On November 25, I didn't really feel like observing my neighbors' buildings with the eyes of a sociologist. The idea came to me later, and once again after an experience of being elsewhere. As I walked through other neighborhoods in Paris, I observed that little by little the flags disappeared. I had the impression that people were taking them down. But every time I came back to my own neighborhood, it all seemed the same as before. Nearly a month ago now, I decided to record the presence of flags, firstly in the neighborhood around the Bataclan and Charlie Hebdo, and then in other neighborhoods of Paris. An overall map has been constructed from these sightings of flags.

These are the maps of the two sectors I documented in their entirety, in the week between March 10 and March 17 (as it happens none of the flags in the neighborhood that I walk through every day have been taken down since). One of these 'islands' of flags is home to a traditionally left-wing electorate (the 11th arrondissement), the other a right-wing electorate (in the 8th arrondissement). One is around the sites of the attacks and the other, around the Champs-Elysées, is much further away.

Firstly, potential visibility appears to be a significant criterion. Many street corners, with multiple viewpoints, give rise to the display of flags. And this can be seen in several different neighborhoods, not just on the maps presented here.

Secondly, there is a kind of conformity that seems to exist in the display of flags. When a road has several flags in it, they are either across from each

153

▲ The Bataclan neighborhood. The sites of the attacks are marked in red. The flags are marked in blue.

other, or in the same building, or in buildings that are close to each other. Keeping up with one's neighbors is a way of seeing and being seen. It is thus more as Parisians and neighbors (rather than as "patriots" or "republicans") that these people have displayed their flags.

Finally, and quite strikingly, when we compare the two maps produced here, it is not only being seen but also seeing and/or having seen that is the explicative criteria for the display of flags.

Several months after the attacks, there are still many flags throughout "Bataclan neighborhood," more than elsewhere, and by far. Living close to the attacks and having seen (again and again), if not the events themselves, then their traces, has clearly encouraged people to put a flag in their window, in spite of the political position that is traditionally less prone to displays of patriotism. Indeed, this is the only neighborhood in which there were so many flags other than French (or the Paris (PSG) football team), such as the Breton or European flags — from the local to the global.

But the importance of seeing and having seen structures the spatial repartition of the display of flags, even within the neighborhood of the attacks.

154

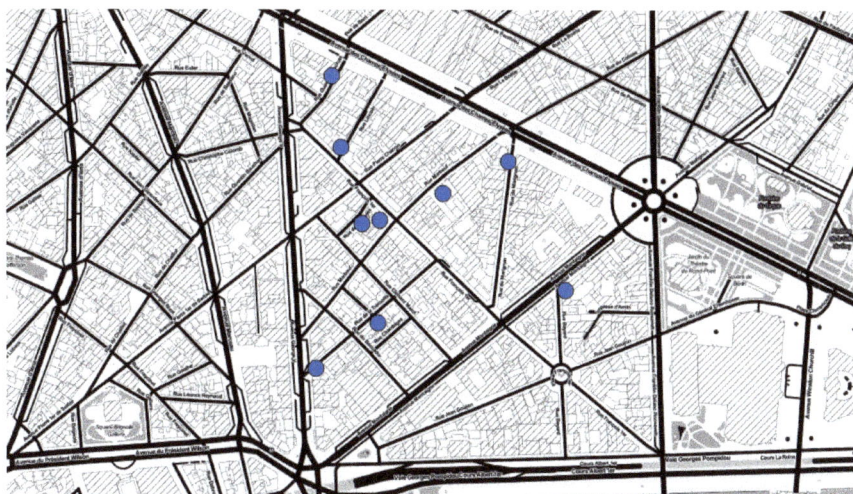

Here flags were counted systematically within the triangle formed by Avenue des Champs-Elysées, Avenue Georges V, and Avenue Montaigne.

The inhabitants that live directly around the sites of the killings display more flags than those whose windows do not look onto the Bataclan, or the building of Charlie Hebdo.

Thus, the part of the Boulevard Voltaire or Passage Saint-Pierre Amelot that give directly onto the concert hall are key sites for the display of flags in windows. Similarly, around the Charlie Hebdo building, there is a greater concentration where the residents saw the siege in the newspaper office. Rue Pelée for example is home to two identical 1970s apartment buildings. At number 7/9, there are seven flags in the windows. At number 17/19, there are none. The Charlie Hebdo offices are visible from the first building, but not from the second.

Randall Collins has shown that, in both San Diego and Philadelphia, the flags put up in solidarity began to be taken down after three months and were completely gone after six months. In Brest, Laurent Le Gall reached the same conclusion.

In Paris this was not the case, still less so in the "Bataclan neighborhood." Beyond the political inclinations and personal motivations of the neighbors who displayed the flags, and whom it remains important to interview, a spatial approach has allowed us to reveal a "neighborhood effect." It encourages us to consider the flag for what it seems to be: a way of displaying one's concern, beyond any particular — or at least univocal — ideological signification.

⌃ Photograph of number 7 Rue Pelée on March 10, 2016. The data collected for this chronical were mapped by Brian Chauvel with help from Cécile Rodrigues, colleagues from the Institute for Social sciences of Politics.

Privatization

May 19, 2016

Last Saturday, May 14, around 6 pm, the polarization of the interpretations of the meanings of the attacks was clearly visible on the Place de la
République, on the fringes of *Nuit Debout*. On the western side, on the bor-
der zone,[1] between the information point of the demonstration, and the memorial for the victims of the attacks, a group of people are painting banners.
They proclaim solidarity and closeness between people of all nationalities
and religions. The American flag appears in the center, on the same level as
those of the other countries touched by terrorism.

1   See "a place to sit", April 8, 2016.

On the eastern fringe, on the other side of *Nuit Debout,* on the edge of Boulevard Voltaire, a completely different discourse is emerging — the denunciation of bombing in Syria by the "Killer State" and the graphic representation of the United States as the nation responsible for these crimes.

Nuit Debout and its general assembly exist between these two extremes. The question of the attacks and how they should be interpreted runs through the movement. The occupation of the public space helps to express this fragmentation of the meaning given to the attacks. This dynamic of fragmentation is reinforced by the fact that it is only a handful of people,[2] only representing themselves,[3] who have been maintaining and arranging the tributes left on the statue since January 2015. Indeed, the state's only intervention in the area has been the planting of the Memory Oak, relegated to the north-west corner of the square, and now looking quite decrepit.[4] The empty space not occupied by official statements, has left room for a privatization, both of memory of the events and the physical surface of the site.

Yesterday, May 18, the Place de la République saw another form of privatization of the public space, which was just as fragmented. Police officers

2   See "Traces", December 31, 2015.

3   See "Property", February 6, 2016.

4   For a picture of this oak see "Property".

staged a demonstration on the square at noon.[5] From 11am onwards, the square was surrounded with barriers, only members of the police force, with their badge, were authorized access. Everyone else was refused entry.

At the barriers, crowds gathered, surprised. Political activists, regular participants in *Nuit Debout*, but also local residents: "This is our square," "the Place has never been closed before," "this is the first time that it's blocked off for one group of people," "it's not their square, it's ours."

The few police officers present congregated on the western side of the Place, the side the least occupied (at night) by *Nuit Debout*, most of whose activities take place on the eastern side. The two movements thus divided the space between themselves, with the statue in the middle, with the memorial at its base. Each in their own "place" — both literally and figuratively.

And because political mobilization operates through the mobilization of the past — on this square more than elsewhere apparently — a new memorial has emerged in response to the police demonstration, now that the square is open again. The zone dedicated to the committees and general assemblies of *Nuit Debout* has been covered by a massive inscription entitled, "They deported our grandparents. They drowned our parents. Everyone hates the police."[6] Underneath, there is a list of a dozen names written in blue, with dates in white, followed by red stencils indicating either "killed" or "mutilated by the police."

5   This was a demonstration against what the police perceive as "hatred of the cops". On the other side, there were people demonstrating against "police violence". These comments refer to the confrontations between demonstrators and police during demonstrations opposing labor reform, which have been held repeatedly since March 2016.

6   "They deported our grandparents" refers to the active participation of the French police in the arrest and deportation of Jews from France during the Holocaust. "They drowned our parents" referred to the fact that during the Algerian war, some of the French police forces drowned some of the Algerian demonstrators in the river Seine in Paris, mostly on October 17, 1961.

Some hours previously, there were heated discussions taking place behind the barriers that prevented access to the square during the police officers' demonstration; discussions between young and old, men and women, between activists and ordinary citizens. The arguments already systematically mobilized both the recent past, and the more distant past, from the 2015 attacks to the Commune, and most often the Second World War, drawing very different conclusions and lessons.

Shift

May 20, 2016

Over the last few weeks, the texts, candles, images and other objects that had been placed around the statue since January 2015 have progressively disappeared. These tributes are now essentially limited to a space on the south side of the statue, at the feet of the lion, where the members of the group *17 Never Again* come each day to (re)arrange this space "for the memory of the victims," as they put it.

Yet, running against this dominant movement, other materials continue to appear here and there on the base, sometimes during visits by school groups.

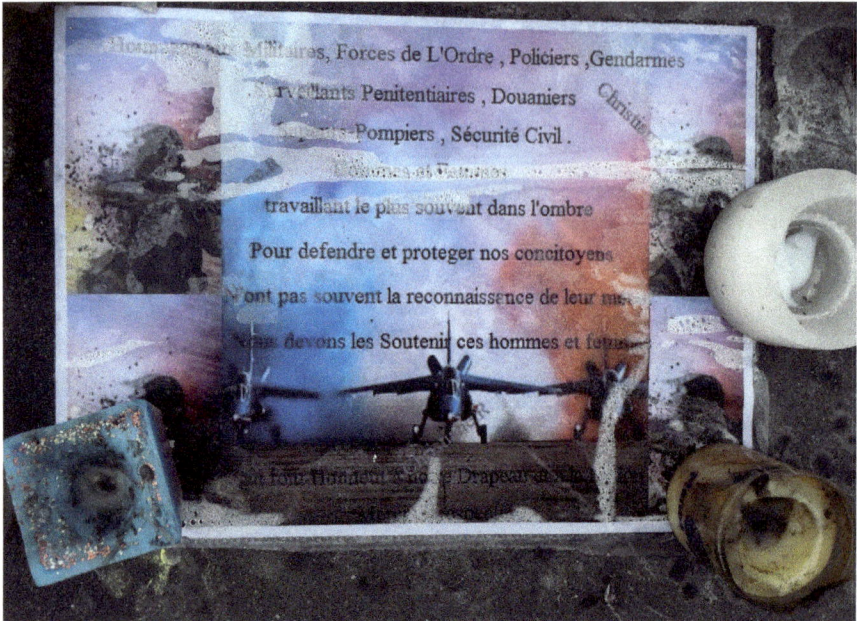

▲ "Homage to the Military, the Security Forces, the Police, the Gendarmes, Prison Guards, Customs Officials, Firefighters, Civil Security. Men and Women working, mostly in the shadows, to defend and protect our fellow citizens, who don't often receive the recognition they deserve. We must support these men and women who honor our flag and our Nation. Respectful Thanks."

On May 20, two new very different kinds of messages attracted my attention. Laminated, and therefore intended to last, they displayed a message in "support of security forces." This theme was previously absent from the memorial and is in profound opposition to the slogans put forward by *Nuit Debout*.

And then I remembered having seen these images on the barriers blocking access to the Place de la République on May 18 during the police demonstration. A man had been holding them in his hand, brandishing them like banners.

He was repeating to anyone who would listen (and those would not) that the police are "just doing their job" and they are "indispensable to our security." It was indeed the attacks and the recent past that were at issue

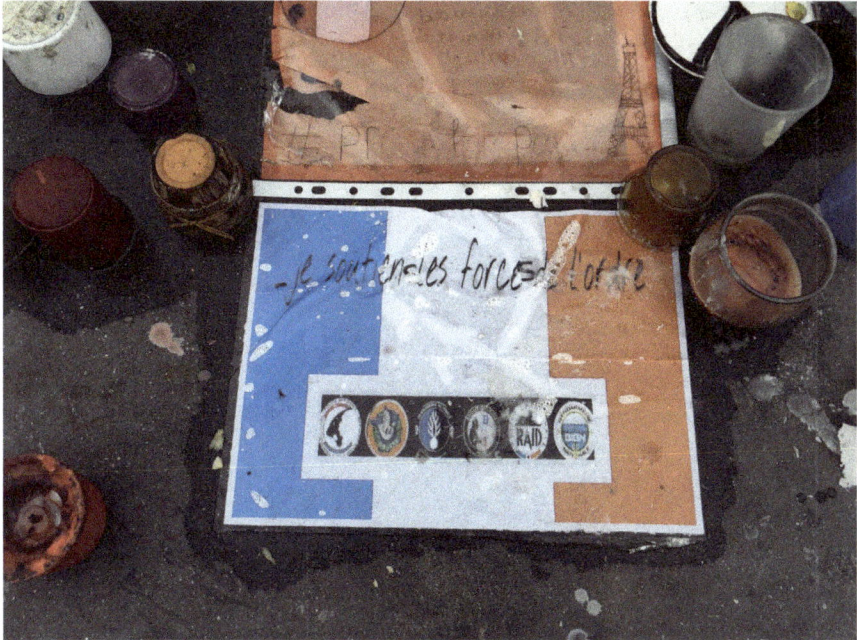

▲ "I support the security forces."

here, as in many other conversations overheard that day. For most of the other people present, the attitudes of the security forces could not be simply reduced to their actions during the attacks. This man was lauding these men and women as being "there to protect the population from attacks."

An internet research suggested that the text and the graphics on these papers were taken from "Honor and Homeland"[1] a non-profit group created in August 2013, in Brittany to "pay homage to the military security forces firemen, customs officials, prison guards civil, security officers, [for] maintaining the cult of remembrance and historic memory, organizing or participating in patriotic ceremonies, defending social and moral interests of members, and encouraging patriotic and civic spirit."

Less imposing than the memorial in homage to those "killed" or "mutilated by the police" which appeared on the ground of the square on the same day, May 18, this message is nevertheless its mirror image. Laminated from the outset, these messages were clearly intended to be a permanent fixture and become part of established memory. Their shift from the edges of the square to the base of the statue further contributes to materializing the symbolic structuring of the space of the Place de la République, on one hand, and the way in which the memory of the attacks coexists with the expression of contemporary social movements, on the other.

---

1   https://fr-fr.facebook.com/honneur-patriecom-226664154063774/.

Banner

May 22, 2016

The summer school holidays are nearly here. The preparations for the end of school celebrations are much talked of between parents at my children's schools. The everyday life of these two schools, situated halfway between the Charlie Hebdo offices and the Bataclan concert hall, is still marked by the events of January and November 2015. Many children are still receiving psychological support, and several families have decided to move away.

It would of course be overly simplistic to only invoke the fear of living in the "Bataclan neighborhood" to explain this situation. Fear is present, of course, but almost implicitly. It is regularly invoked as a specter that must be fought against. This week, on several different occasions, fighting fear and celebrating life were presented to me as being the two main motivations for moving ahead with the organization of an end of year school celebration.

It is thus particularly striking that it was also this week that a major symbol of the memorial on the Place de la République disappeared. From January 7, 2015, immediately after the massacre of the cartoonists at Charlie Hebdo, several celebrities had put up a banner on the base of the statue with the clear message — "Même Pas Peur" ("You Don't Scare Us"). Initially this banner was improvised from marker pens on a piece of white fabric.

From the very moment it was put up, and for as long as it was the largest most visible message on the statue, this banner continued to change. I even considered dedicating a chronicle to its evolution, on Thursday May 19, which would have looked at the changes to the banner as a symbol of the evolution of the memorial itself. It was with this idea in mind that I went to see it on May 20, 2016, only to find that it had disappeared. This of course makes it all the more relevant to trace the steps the led up to its removal.

▲ Photograph of the banner in its initial form, taken here on December 20, 2015. © MB

The first modification of the banner reflects the memorial's shift from ephemeral spontaneity to heritage. A year after its impromptu appearance, and after the national commemorations of January 2016, the same artists and comedians came back to the site. They left the original banner but covered it with a new one that can be described as for "posterity." This new version carried the same message but with improved graphics written on more resistant, more weatherproof material, intended to last and to continue the commemoration in the long term.

Confirmed as being a salient point of the memorial, the banner reflected the evolutions of the social and political content that were expressed on the Place de la République, from March onward, in the context of the demonstrations against labor reforms. In this respect, it symbolized the inter-connectedness of the two causes, the memorialization of the attacks on one hand and the social struggle on the other. Thus, on March 7, 2016, before *Nuit Debout* appeared, I noticed the appearance of the slogan "liberty and fantasy." Fantasy was written in the continuation of the original message while liberty echoed the context immediately surrounding the demonstrations, and the encirclement of the memorial by metal barriers.[1]

1   See "Conflict", Mars 17 2016.

166

Some weeks later, just as terrorism struck another major European town, Brussels, the return of the climate of fear was reflected on the banner. Underneath the initial slogan, someone had written the word "mytho" ("liar") in large letters.

Then, on May 4, I suddenly realized that the original banner, which had previously remained underneath the new weatherproof one, had disappeared. The banner thus moved away from its original association with the memorial to be transformed into the Banner for the causes of various participants in *Nuit Debout,* which had by then been in place for a month.

It was associated with the critique of consumerism (on the left), the affirmation of political struggles (with the black sticker on the lower right-hand side "Black Mamba: Parisian-style Antifascism") and the condemnation of the financial system (with the green stick in support of Greece).

On May 11, a final message appeared on the banner: "*Vive Algérie, Tunisie, Maroc*" ("*long live Algeria, Tunisia, Morocco,*" on the upper right-hand side). This reference to France's former colonies and protectorates in the

167

Maghreb would find a disturbing echo a week later in the immense memorial to those "killed by the police."[2] This memorial would cover the east side of the square in reaction to the demonstration by police officers. Indeed, the reference to the Algerians drowned by the police during the demonstrations for Algerian independence on October 17, 1961 in Paris is central here.

The evolution of the banner between January 2015 and May 2016 thus documents the shift from a movement in reaction to the attacks, to other social movements for various causes. Yet all of these are expressed on the space of the banner.

What then should we conclude from its recent disappearance? Is this the symbol of an incompatibility between the memorialization of the attacks and the affirmation of contemporary social struggles? Is it a sign of some peoples' desire to return to fear? Or does it mark the end of the memorial function of the statue?

On May 20, the day that I noticed the banner's disappearance, I spoke with a member of the group *17 Never Again,* who was organizing things around the south face of the pedestal. Students from French class at a protestant high school in the United States had just come to add many drawings and messages to the memorial, and my interlocutor was photographing them. He would then protect them and arrange them, and possibly store them at his own house.

I told him about the disappearance of the banner and asked him if his group was responsible. He was surprised and angry. "It's not there? That's incredible! You know, it's the people from *Nuit Debout.* There are people who are totally out of it. We were assaulted the other day. That's what it's like. But here I'm taking photos of all these drawings. Look, there are things on both sides." He broke off and turned toward me "We are working for memory here."

But what memory, and whose memory, is that?

2   See "Privatization" May 19, 2016.

More than anything, the space left by the banner reveals the veritable lack of a collective interpretation — even a controversial one — of the 2015 attacks in Paris. It sheds light on the absence of the state (or any political representation, national or local) in the management of this ephemeral memorial. As a result, there is indeed a form of privatization of the public space that was established even before the demonstration by police officers, and before *Nuit Debout* emerged.

Sacred

May 24, 2016

My daughter normally stays at school to have lunch at the canteen, but on May 24 she came home to eat. At 1.30pm, after I had taken her back for afternoon classes, I walked home past the Bataclan for the second time that day. I noticed a bouquet of flowers that hadn't been there earlier in the morning. It was blue and red, and on the sash was written "Paris City Council." It was the sign of an official visit.

So, I decided to remain close by to see what was going to happen. Around 2pm, several cars with tinted windows arrived. I slowly understood that a delegation from the *"Orient et Occident — Civilisations en dialog"* (*East and West — civilizations in dialog*) conference, held that morning at the City Hall had decided to come to the Bataclan. Among them were Ahmed el-Tayeb, the Grand Imam of al-Azhar, and Andrea Riccardi the founder of the Catholic community Sant'Egidio. Together they laid a wreath alongside the one laid by the Mayor. Its colors stood out next to the more traditional colors of the Republic and instead of the tricolor sash there was a small piece of white paper.

On this paper was a handwritten message from the Grand Imam Ahmed el-Tayeb, which is translated below. It calls for peace and dialog.

It is not my hand that is holding the folded paper in this photograph, but one of the participants in the East and West meeting. Indeed, once Ahmed el-Tayeb had left, the members of the delegation, especially those from the "East" picked up the message one by one to take photos of it and of them-selves holding it.

Much like a sacred object, a relic, this paper was passed from hand to hand along the footpath and many photos were taken of it — undoubtedly

1. *The first line is difficult to translate, it seems to evoke a traditional prayer used to accompany an important action.*

2. "I am here to say, in the name of Islam, that it is forbidden to spill the blood of any man."

3. "That the relation between all men, that God asked of us, is a relation of peace, fraternity and mutual assistance (solidarity)."

4. "That terrorism has neither homeland nor religion."

5. "All Muslims are very moved by each drop of blood that was spilled here and elsewhere because of this dangerous plague."

6. "Our duty both in the East and the West, is to unite against this plague."

7. "I am deeply moved for these victims, for their families, and their friends."

8. "I hope that the French people, free and open, will be able to continue on after this tragedy."

9. "May God protect you and protect us from all these woes."

10. "Signature Ahmed Tayeb — cheikh d'AL-Azhar — Director of the Muslim Assembly, 24/ 05/2016"

▲ Translation of the text that disappeared, line by line, by OBI and DBI (thank you!)

destined for the internet. Several passersby stopped to watch the scene and to try to understand what was happening. Among them, I noticed a member of the group *17 Never Again*, as well as several other people I often see in the neighborhood.

As we have seen in other chronicles, the tributes — messages, photos, objects and even sometimes dried flowers — that are left at the Bataclan, are destined for conservation at the Paris Archives. However, this tiny piece of paper, so laded with symbolism, would never make it to the collections, to be preserved among the thousands of other texts already in the archives. By 6pm, only three hours after the previous scene, on my way back from picking my daughter up, this small piece of paper was nowhere to be seen. I searched in vain, but clearly someone had taken it. This handwritten text by Ahmed el-Tayeb was lost for posterity, even though its highly symbolic nature was clearly intended to constitute a "historic" message.

Trauma

June 13, 2016

Yesterday there was a shooting in a popular gay nightclub in Orlando, Florida.[1] Like many others, I immediately began to search for information about it on the internet. This reaction provoked another, just as impulsive, from my partner: "Stop! What are you doing? There is nothing to learn. It already happened on your doorstep. There's no point reliving it all." Do events like this repeat themselves?

For many, the recent massacre has undoubtedly revived the memory of the shootings at the Bataclan and probably also the stress we experienced in

1   In the night of June 12, 2016, the day of Gay Pride, a man opened fire in a crowded night club in Orlando, Florida, popular with the LGBT community. 50 people were killed. Islamic State later claimed responsibility for the attack.

174

November 2015. Journalists and documentary makers are once again every-where in our neighborhood, preparing for the first anniversary of the at-tacks: asking whether the neighborhood has been changed, to what extent it is "traumatized" or "resilient."

The attacks are of course now part of the everyday lives of those who live here; they interfere here and there in our conversations, and sometimes take up residence in our silences. One evening, not long ago, my daughter questioned me about "our" risk of being flooded by the rising flood waters of the Seine.[2] I replied "No, you know we're too far away from the river," and then, tired from a long day, I added without thinking "and, you know, enough already!" And then silence, I didn't elaborate. But my daughter didn't miss a beat and returned "Yes you're right *Maman*! We already had the attacks!" The meaning of my "enough" was perfectly clear for her. She clearly has the attacks on her mind too. But does that mean she is traumatized?

My son, who is only four, apparently considers the new face of our neigh-borhood since November to be completely "normal." For him, police officers, tourists and journalists[3] have become ordinary figures on our streets. On Saturday June 4, we were waiting for the "Tropical Carnival" parade to come down the Boulevard du Temple.[4] At the head of the parade there were around thirty police officers in combat uniform. My son turned toward me with a huge smile and said — "*Maman*, you didn't say there'd be a police carnival too!! That's so cool!"

2   At the beginning of June 2016, the Seine river flooded in Paris. At its peak, the river reached 6m10, a level which had not been reached since January 1982. I took my children to the banks of the river to see the water rise.

3   See the chronicles entitled "Tourism" (January 5) and "Journalists" (March 7, 2016).

4   On Saturday June 4, the 15th Tropical Carnival was held in Paris. After leaving from the Town Hall, the parade went through the 3rd and 4th arrondissements, up to the Boulevard des Filles du Calvaire, crossing the Place de la République. Originally created by the Caribbean community in Paris to showcase their herit-age, the carnival now includes many cultures from all around the world.

▲ Flyers presenting the project 13–11, laid out on the counter of my local pharmacy.

What should we make of the legitimate considerations of this "trauma" and its opposite "resilience," both of the "neighborhood" and/or the "residents" as a group — a trauma whose existence seems to be taken for granted by many commentators? There are even research programs that seek to measure the size and understand the nature of this "trauma" and "resilience." Yet the definition of trauma, like that of resilience, lies in the realm of the psyche and is the province of psychiatrists, psychologists and other analysts. Its source is thus within the individual.

A "neighborhood," its streets, its buildings and even the society, or societies, that its inhabitants might constitute, have no brain, no psyche. They have no conscious, no sub-conscious. Many sociologists, including myself, therefore struggle with the definition of a "collective" trauma, and even more so with the ways in which its existence and its effects may be observed. We therefore focus more on the social relations that connect the individuals who constitute this "collective."

176

Last week, the attacks were at the heart of two separate conversations that I had in the course of a single day, with two mothers of my children's friends. Each time, one of the starting points was the call for testimonies, launched by the CNRS and INSERM for the "November 13"[5] program. On this particular occasion, the message had been sent out by the school, but flyers advertising this research program are visible all over the neighborhood — in the shops, in the parks and in the council buildings.

The two mothers I spoke to both live across the road from the Bataclan (one outside its entrance, the other outside the exit), they are both in relationships, have young sons and work full-time. They both describe themselves as "overcome" with emotion by the night of November 13; indeed, for both of them the memory of that night is still present today, still raw and still stressful. Their feelings (naturally it is not for me to describe them as traumatic) seem similar, if not the same. Yet does that mean they reflect a "collective" or "shared" impact of the attacks?

One of them wanted to speak publicly about her experience, to bear witness; the other prefers to scribble it all down in a notebook she intends to keep to herself. The first signed up to participate in the research program to collect peoples' stories of the night of November 13, run by the CNRS and INSERM. The other considered the very idea intrusive.

Indeed, their distinct reactions to the act of testifying about their experiences, their suffering, are accompanied by very different social practices. This is true for example, in the context of the neighborhood itself; the first has decided to move house, move away from the edges of the concert hall. In contrast, the second has intensified her connection to the local community; she has for example tried to motivate people so that this year the annual

---

5   The "November 13" research program is a cross-disciplinary program that will evolve over 12 years. Its objective is to study the construction and the evolution of the memory of November 13 2015, whilst also conceptualizing the articulations between memory and collective memory, http://www.memoire13novembre.fr. The research teams conduct campaigns to collect testimonies and experiences from the residents of the neighborhood among other groups ("victims", "Parisians" and "French people").

school party will take place "in spite of everything," to "celebrate life." But it is also true for their professional lives as well. The first works in an intellectual profession and is used to speaking in public and speaking in the first person. The second works in the service sector, in a profession that requires discretion and where voicing one's own opinion is out of place.

It therefore seems difficult to define and delimit a "collective trauma," which could be seen as characteristic of the neighborhood. Yet I do see, every day a little more, that for these "residents'" — who are for me first and foremost "neighbors" — the expression of their experiences indeed constitutes a social phenomenon. It is framed by a range of social relations and situations. This observation is both a sign of the undeniable impact of the events, and a sign that this impact has not radically overhauled the society of our neighborhood. On the contrary, it is in the context of this society, a genuine social framework that at least partially existed before the attacks, that the impact of these events finds its form and unfolds.

▲ Photo taken on June 13, 2016, in the Passage Saint-Pierre Amelot, where the emergency exit of the Bataclan comes out. The bullet holes are still visible but the graffiti "express yourself" (photographed on June 2) has been painted over.

Color

June 14, 2016

Last night, the link between *Nuit Debout* and the attacks emerged once again on the space of the Place de la République. Echoing the general assemblies that marked the high points of the movement, and in response to a call from its organizers, a gathering was held in homage to the victims of the homophobic attack in Orlando. New drawings and messages were left on the base of the statue.

The tributes left on the sites of the attacks in November have, for the most part, been collected by the Paris Archives which is now responsible for preserving them. But this is not the case for the tributes left on the place de la République, where there is still no official archival policy. In any case, even when they are preserved, they are forever separated from the context in which they were left. It is generally impossible to know who left them and under what circumstances.

In a previous chronicle[1] I was able to make a connection between a text that was left in front of the Bataclan, and the identity and intention of the person who left it. Yesterday evening, my colleague Sylvain Antichan was present at the Place de la République. He observed and interviewed several participants. One young couple left a paper banner made of paper that read "The more you kill us, the more we will love each other." Sylvain was able to talk to them to provide some context for this tribute.

The man, aged 26, and the woman, aged 23, were both philosophy students. They arrived in Paris in September 2015 from Portugal (she is Portuguese, and he is Belgian-Portuguese) and they now live in the 18th arrondissement. They regularly attend the *Nuit Debout* meetings and listen to the work of the committees, even though they have never taken an active part in the movement. They said that they were particularly sensitive to issues around LGBT rights. That night they had come in response to the attack in Orlando and brought the banner in the photograph above. They chose the place to hang it with care. The man wanted it to be hung next to the Franco-Belgian tribute, as though it were an echo of his own national belongings. The place they chose was also on the edge of the sector dedicated to the memorial. This was the first time that either of them had come here to leave a tribute after an attack. For the attacks in Brussels, the young man said he had been "too involved," he "called people" and "didn't even think" (of coming here). For Paris, in November, "we had just arrived" in the capital. They made their banner "an hour ago, in a park nearby", and they "brought the supplies from home."

How can we describe this banner? As a political message or an expression of compassion? And which attack does it refer to? Orlando of course, but perhaps also Brussels, and even Paris? Finally, could participation in the

---

1   See the chronicle entitled "Interpretation" (January 8, 2016).

memorialization of the attacks in the public space be particularly the province of individuals situated at a precise distance — both geographical and affective — from these dramatic events? Neither too far, nor too close?

Indeed, I realize, as I write these lines, that among our neighbors (even though a systematic survey has yet to be conducted) no one has ever mentioned leaving a tribute at the Place de la République or any of the other sites.

Nor have I or my partner.

However, our children did leave candles at the Place de la République on the evenings of January 7 and November 15, 2016.

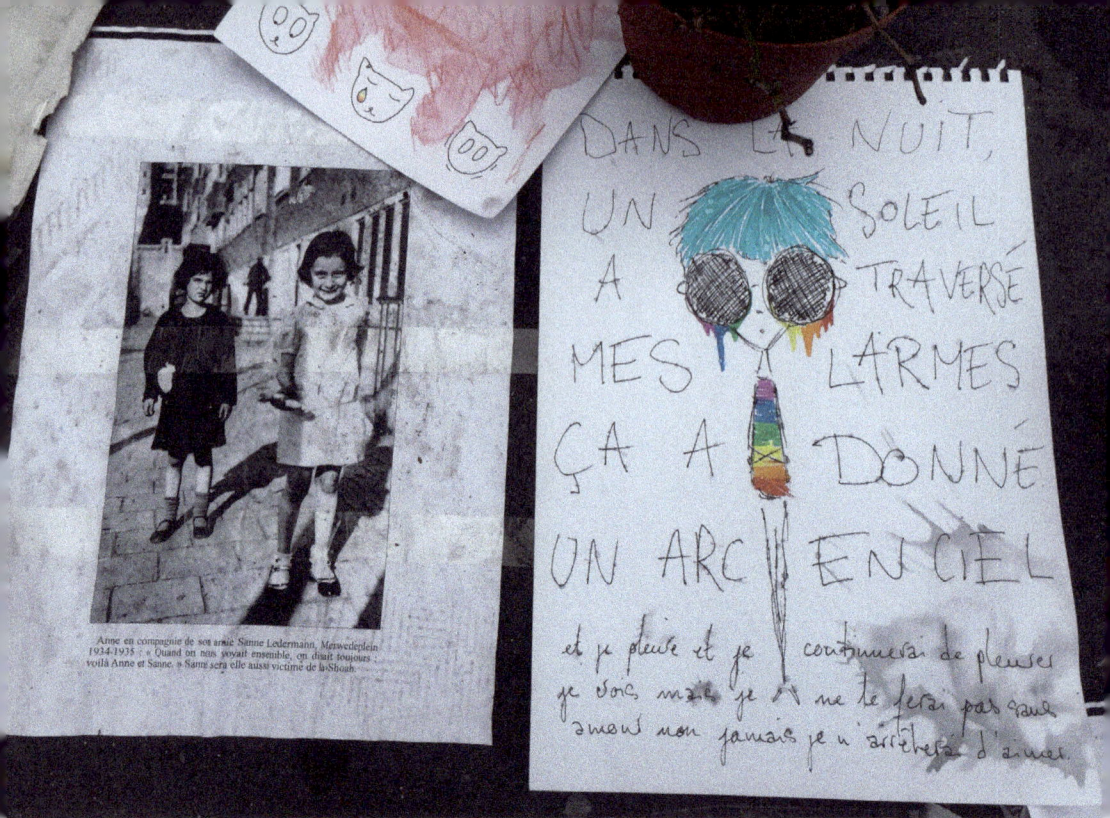

Icons

June 18, 2016

The rain has washed away the color from many of the tributes and messages. Black and white has now replaced the rainbow.

On the left of these photos, taken yesterday and the day before, the flyer of Anne Frank is one of around twenty others that have recently appeared in reference to the iconic Jewish girl.

A reference like this is atypical. Ultimately very few of the documents left up until now on the place de la République have explicitly referred to the Second World War, and the extermination of the Jews. This is less true for

182

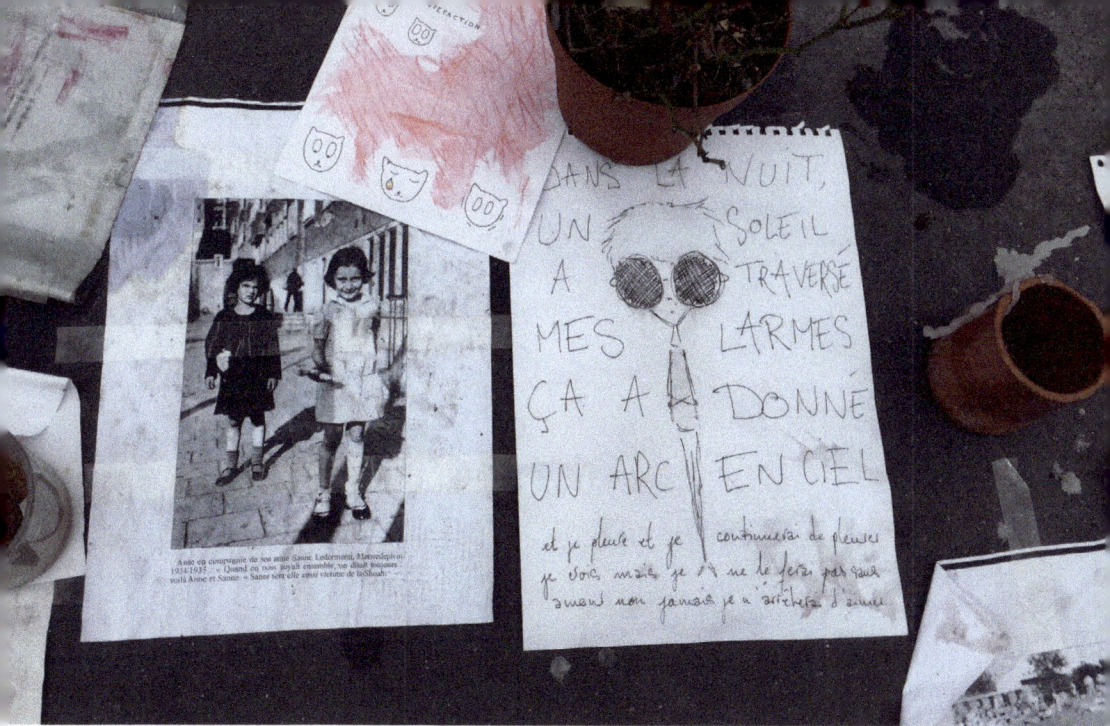

the tributes left around the Bataclan, where such references seem to be more frequent.[1]

Today the references to Anne Frank have disappeared. In their place, on the lion, two posters have been set up in homage to the victims of the recent attack in Orlando, and the attack in Magnanville, where two French police officers were murdered.[2] In fact it is the only sign of solidarity with the police that is visible on the statue.

1   It is important to note that there were many traditional Jewish candles left regularly at the sites (see the Chronicle entitled "Pilgrimage"). On January 9, 2015 there was an attack on a Jewish supermarket in the east of Paris in which a gunman held shoppers hostage, resulting in four people killed and two others wounded. The fact that the site of this shooting was on the edge of Paris, near the towns of Saint-Mandé and Vincennes, partly explains why it is less present in this fieldwork, which focuses on my "doorstep" in the 11th district. This will be discussed in more detail in the conclusion of this book.

2   On June 13, 2016, a police officer and his wife (who worked at the Ministry of the Interior) were killed at their home by a man who claimed to be working for the Islamic State. The killer was shot by police during the assault.

The form of these messages (laminated, with gray masking tape and hearts) but especially the slogan that is used, which became iconic after "*Je suis Charlie*," seems to suggest that is was the members of the group *17 Never Again* who put them up. Even the reaction to the attacks now has its own norms, standards and icons.

Preaching

June 18, 2016

I have lived in the neighborhood for a little more than eight years now and I have always seen preachers here — most often Jehova's Witnesses. Always in pairs, a man and a woman, they stand in the same place, on the edge of the Place de la République, but not quite on it, at the exit of the metro "Rue du Temple." But in the last few days they have instead taken up position in the middle of the square, clearly desirous to occupy this public space that has indeed become a place for the preaching of beliefs and convictions.

Today, a group of Mormon missionaries, mostly Americans living in France, have also set up in the middle of the Place. Although not normally

185

subversive, they have adapted to the usage of the site and drawn the main symbols of their theology on the ground of the north side of the square.

I talked to one of them. Originally from Arizona, he began by explaining to me at length the notions of "paradise," "prison" and the other fundamental elements for the Mormons. He asked if I had faith and assured me that Jesus Christ could help me in these difficult times.

I told him that I lived nearby and that it was the first time that I had seen so many of their group on the square. He explained what I already knew, "ordinarily we work in pairs and it is much more discrete." He then added, "but we thought that the paradise of the Mormons could be useful for the people who have been coming to the Place de la République since the attacks and we decided to do something different here."

"Why are we here?" asked the missionaries on that day, while taking a group photograph. The implication of their question was "here on this earth," on a theological level, but in the context of the symbolism of this site, the question becomes figurative and the "here" takes on a new meaning.

Reconquest

June 19, 2016

On June 17, in the evening, an advertising column and billboards appeared on the Place de la République. These urban structures were designed to be used in an exhibition organized by the Paris City Council and the High Commission for Refugees. The goal was to create an exhibition of portraits of refugees, and (I imagine) to encourage Parisians to want to welcome them.

For anyone who has been observing the Place over the last few months this appearance will seem to be a sign of the Council's desire to reconquer the public space. It is accompanied by the recent cleaning and re-opening of the toy library[1] on the square, at maximum capacity this morning. Initially set up when the square was made a pedestrian space, since the attacks the toy library had only been partially open, until now.

---

1   The targeted audience being both residents and tourists or passersby.

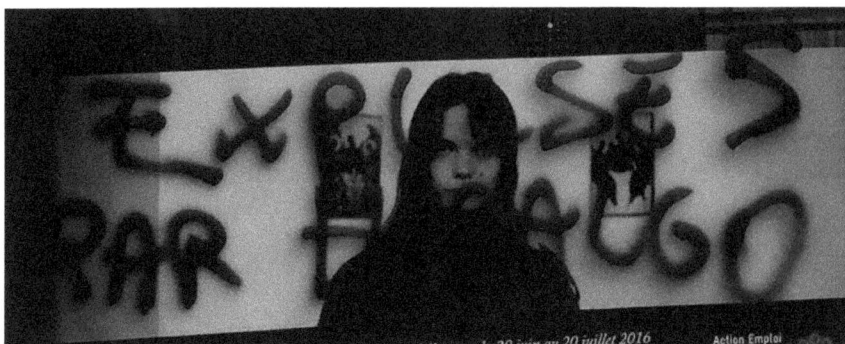

Setting up this exhibition space also confirms the symbolic distribution of the space of the Place de la République. The west side of the square is the space for the authorities and the institutions, national as well as municipal. Other than this exhibition which uses traditional urban infrastructure, this is also the part of the square where the Memory Oak and the commemorative plaque, inaugurated by François Hollande in January 2016, are. It is also where the café (which is a concession of the City Council) is, now named after the official motto of Paris "Fluctuat Nec Mergitur,"[2] and where the police demonstration was held on May 18. By contrast, the eastern side has remained a space of contestation and political subversion.

It is therefore not surprising that as early as yesterday morning, several posters had been graffitied with messages criticizing the Council's policy: "deported by [Mayor] Hildago," "deported everyday," "Refugees in Paris *on the street* (added)".

But by this morning (Sunday), these slogans had been removed.

On the Place, the forms of reconstruction of the public space clearly still need to be found; the space may remain non-consensual but may not *necessarily* be always cleaved in two as seems to be the case now.

2   "She is tossed by the waves but does not sink."

Flags

June 27, 2016

Since yesterday morning, the Council's reconquering of the Place de la République has continued. A range of new structures for discovering different sporting activities now occupies the whole square. For several weeks now, the neighborhood has been dressed up in soccer colors. Although République doesn't have an official "fan zone" to host spectators of the European cup (which started in France on June 10) it is an attraction for fans, both French and foreigners. One Swedish family for example visited the "memorial" for the attacks before their national team's game. In keeping with the mood, the residents have hung national colors here and there throughout the neighborhood.

A Swedish flag was draped over a balcony on Boulevard Voltaire. Five buildings further along, there is a French flag. The first disappeared after the elimination of the Swedish team at the end of the first round. The second remains.

In the neighborhood, flags of other countries thus now hang alongside the French tricolor which was initially displayed as a reaction to the attacks and which have largely been left in the windows ever since. This seems to be particular to this part of Paris, as we saw in the chronicle "Seeing" (May 13). Sometimes this means several flags are hung together, as was the case in this building of the nearby 3rd arrondissement on June 17 on the eve of one of the Portuguese national team's games: a French one for the attacks (on the right shutter) and a Portuguese for the European cup (on the left and on the windows).[1]

But these new usages of the flag also have an impact on the French tricolor. Since I have taken to looking up, to observe people's windows, my daughter has adopted the habit of pointing out "new flags" as she says. In these last two weeks, she has — rightly — noticed the appearance of several of them, on sidewalk cafés of course, but also on buildings. I explained to her that "those flags are there for the football, not for the attacks." But on the other hand, I noticed the disappearance of several flags that were previously displayed, as though for certain residents the appearance of the "other" (soccer) flags (French and otherwise) for the 2016 UEFA European Football Championship, detracted from, or altered, the meaning(s) of their own display. The specific situation in the neighborhood is a good illustration of the multiplicity of meanings that can be associated with a single flag.

1   Clearly well before the final between France and Portugal.

▲ Photographs taken in June and March 2016 respectively.[2]

Sometimes this superposition of the meanings can be seen in a single window. This large tricolor has hung in this window since November, but just recently another has been added, in honor of the Euro Cup — one above the blinds, the other underneath them. A café in the neighborhood, which I walk past every day, also displays this same polysemy. The flag displayed in November in the window is now covered by another flag — celebrating the Euro Cup. The question remains whether it is indeed relevant to separate the flags into two categories (as I did with my daughter) — those for the attacks and those for the football. The French flags in place since November have undoubtedly found a new echo in the sporting decorations. Inversely, in a neighborhood where the French flag has been ever present since the terrorist attacks, hanging a French flag in support of the national team cannot completely overlook the new meaning and association the tricolor has acquired in recent months.

2   On November 11, 2016, the date I finished the manuscript for the French version of this book, the flag was still hanging in this window.

Empty
July 1, 2016

Yesterday evening, several of the display cases for exhibition on the refugees in Paris had been vandalized and the glass smashed. Today, the exhibition has been removed and the western side of the Place is now empty. The exhibition was initially supposed to continue until July 20. Reconquering the Place is not an easy task. This is a reminder that the city is not just a material reality but also, and even above all, an ensemble of social relations, which are themselves inscribed in power relations.

▲ © SA

Date

July 16, 2016

For several weeks now, I have considered bringing these chronicles to an end. This daily observation of my environment, as a sociologist of memory, has enabled me to "live with" the violence[1] that took place here, and which I experienced as a resident of this part of the 11th arrondissement. The perspective of leaving the neighborhood for the summer holidays also seems to me to be the opportunity to turn the page — both literally and figuratively — and finish my writings on the traces of the events, at least in this form.

July 14, France's national holiday, seemed an "natural" choice for the final date for these chronicles. "Naturally" is however a particularly "unnatural" term for a sociologist. This choice was based on two factors. On one hand, it seemed to me that July 14 was the day when, every year, many Parisians begin to leave Paris for holidays elsewhere — even though my own family and I would still be in Paris on that day. On the other hand, I now realize (retrospectively) that July 14 also marked for me the end of a period, a kind of return to normal, a semblance of confidence in the ability of French political society to hold fast. The full awareness of this symbolic charge, and its largely illusionary foundation, did not become clear to me until I saw them in the light of the killing that took place in Nice, on that very night, during the fireworks celebrating July 14, 2016.[2]

In my neighborhood, which had returned to a kind of normality recently, this new massacre led to a renewal of the tributes on the one hand, and a

---

1   See the chronicle by the same name of December 27, 2015.

2   On July 15, 2014, during the fireworks celebrating the national day, a man drove a large truck into the crowd over several meters, killing nearly one hundred people and leaving hundreds of others wounded.

social mobilization in the public space on the other. Yesterday evening, a crowd gathered to leave messages and French flags on the base of the statue, while the members of the group *17 never again* (who had retired over recent weeks) immediately came (back) to organize the space.

∧ The blond lady has returned.

During these last two days, the same actions and messages seen previously have been repeated. The cartoonist Liox has once again left a drawing of Marianne, people have returned to write "*Je suis*" and "*Pray for*," this time followed by "*Nice*." Others have relit their candles, or once again drawn flags, such as the Kabyle flag, as has been regular practice here since January 2015.

And in the crowd, new (or old) causes have again been remembered in the memorial. Yesterday afternoon, demonstrators unrolled a huge banner against "terrorism in Bangladesh," accompanied by French and Bangladeshi flags. Today there was a crowd supporting the President Erdogan, waving Turkish flags, but who said they were "also there for Nice." Indeed, the youngest went constantly back and forth between the official memorial and the west side of the statue (the legitimist side) where

195

the demonstration against the *coup d'Etat* was held.[3] On the east side of the square, activists from *Nuit Debout* organized a new workshop hijacking advertisements, while, earlier in the day, some of their fellows had painted new frescos on the ground, in light of the events.

Sociologists talk about "saturation point" to describe the moment when the collection of new material (interviews, observations, archives, statistics) simply confirms the conclusions and analytic categories that the previous material had provided. For research in the field, the observation of this mechanism is the sign that the fieldwork can stop. The repetition that we observe here is thus the confirmation that these chronicles, and this type of limited and evidential research,[4] can soon come to an end.

But it is now impossible for July 14 to be the date of the final chronicle. It is now in itself the date of a new event.

3   An attempted coup, ultimately averted, took place in Turkey during the night of July 15–16, 2016.

4   This expression refers to Carlo Ginzburg's work (1989).

Silence

July 24, 2016

The same pattern repeats itself. However, the extent of the killings in Nice has had particular, implicit resonance for my partner and me. The event had a profound impact on us, even though it remained, in part, distant.

Of course, my family and I, like our friends and neighbors, were all horrified by the massacres. How could we not be? But this time, the distance — both geographical and social — from the events in Nice, made us painfully conscious of our violent proximity to the attacks in Paris in January, and then November 2015. Since July 14 we have been living through a strange repetition of events, blended with a radical difference. The walls of the neighborhood testify as to this shift, and the retrospective understanding that, henceforth, "November 13" will take on new meaning knowing that it was followed by a "July 14."

After November 13, 2015, residents of the neighborhood displayed the flag[1] proudly in apartment windows or outside shops — some are still there. Originally the tricolor was intended to show a kind of solidarity or concern. Today, these flags seem to be part of the background. And this time, it is in fact when they are brought down, to half-mast, as a sign of mourning, that they represent a social reaction to the recent attack in Nice.

On Monday July 18, a minute of silence was organized at the Place de la République. In January and November 2015, it would never have occurred to me to go to such a gathering. Far removed from the massive spontaneous tribute events that took place after those attacks, we were immersed in chaos and cacophony and in the need to connect with each other, and these dominated.

---

1   See the chronicle entitled "See", 13 May and "Flags", June 27, 2016.

▲ Private flag at half-mast outside a shop on Boulevard Beaumarchais. Photographed on July 16.

At noon on January 8, 2015, during the official minute of silence for the Charlie Hebdo shootings, I was at the head office of the National Center for Scientific Research (CNRS), in the 16th arrondissement in Paris. I had been attending a meeting and it was thus collectively, as a professional group, that we all went down into the foyer of the building, to be silent.

Last Monday, I was home alone. I would not have gone alone to the Place de la République as a resident. Instead I went as a sociologist, and only this once. There were at most sixty people there. They were holding hands. The contrast between this and the huge crowds that had appeared here during the previous attacks — which were both in Paris and in this very neighborhood — was striking.

More and more often the reactions to a particular attack make spontaneous reference to other events.[2] Thus, at the base of the memorial, passersby have written *"we are Nice"* on a Belgian flag, thus also referring to the attacks in Brussels. On the lion, a woman has hung a Coptic cross with a message in Arabic. She speaks English, she says she is a refugee from Egypt who has come here in solidarity with the victims of the Nice attack, to explain that the Copts in Egypt are victims too, of the same kind of violence "but nobody is interested." And in this new context of sometimes violent, racist or discriminatory reactions against Muslims, the reappearance of religious candles strikes me once again. What did the person who left a votive in the name of "Sainte Rita Nice" want to say?

The reactions to the attacks have provided opportunities to take stances and make speeches, to defend causes and make claims. They are far from silent.

2   See the chronicle entitled "Colors", June 14, 2016.

Ephemeral

August 1, 2016

Today we leave Paris for the "big holidays" as the children put it. We'll be back in three weeks.

I decide to visit the place de la République one last time before my departure. It is 9.30 in the morning and the statue is surrounded by a metal fence blocking access. In front of the fence, a man whom I recognize as being a member of the group *17 Never Again*, is watching the council workers at their tasks. I strike up a conversation with him, as I have often seen him here. "They came without telling us you know. Apparently they came at five o'clock in the morning. Secretly. I was still here at 11pm last night." A woman, on the other side of the fence, was listening to our conversation.

She approached us and interrupted "Not 5am, Monsieur, 8.30am. There was no secrecy about it. Before we arrived, the Paris Archives came and took away some posters and drawings." The man remained silent and walked off around the statue.

The Paris City Council has thus decided to make the most of the summer to clean the site and regain control over it. The previous attempts to reconquer the space, first (again with the intermediary of the metal barriers[1]) shortly before "Nuit Debout" appeared, and then with the photography exhibition about refugees,[2] both failed. The lull in activity that accompanies the month of August in Paris should mean the operation is more successful this time.

1   See the chronicle entitled "Demonstration", March 10, 2016.

2   See the chronicle entitled "Empty", July 1, 2016.

The question remains open, however, as to whether the established uses of the statue will in fact disappear. The English expression "grassroots memorial" (Margry & Sánchez-Carretero, 2011) has been translated into French as "ephemeral memorial" (*memorial éphémère*), and it is clear why this translation is problematic. A memorial that is fed by passersby, who leave flowers, texts, drawings, photos, flags and candles cannot be assumed to be ephemeral. It can last. In this case, it has lasted 19 months!

It can also disappear and then reappear. This kind of memorial can no longer be defined by a criterion of duration, or even of material fragility. Rather, once again, it must be defined by its place in a space of social relations and power relationships. It is thus distinctive in the fact that it is not an "official memorial," set up by a state, an association or any other unified cause.

Indeed occasionally, the two types of memorial can share a single space, as in the case of the Vietnam Veterans Memorial in Washington D.C. Despite its very solemn and official nature, people continue to leave various spontaneous tributes and homages here. Robin Wagner-Pacific and Barry Schwartz have studied thousands of letters, candles and objects that are still left here every day. Through their practices, these visitors have thus constructed an individual and private connection with the commemorated past, while also simultaneously participating in its public and collective celebration (Wagner-Pacifici & Barry Schwartz, 1995).

Inversely, does the decision to raze the memorial on the Place de la République mean that the city has decided to construct an official site for commemoration — in response to the demands of several orangizations?[3] For the moment, the municipal representatives who were there for the setting up of the barriers and the beginning of the cleaning, were directing people to the Memory Oak[4] on the far west side of the Place, before stressing that the Paris Archives had collected the tributes.

3   http://generationbataclan.fr/Vote/.
4   See the chronicle entitled "Reflections", January 10, 2016.

The previous chronicles have, however, shown that this collection took place everywhere except on the Place de la République, which was left to the responsibility of the group 17 *Never Again*. Yet, since January 2015, this is where most of the tributes have been left. They also lead us to hypothesize that the documents collected by the Paris Archives this morning will not be the last to be left here.

Each anniversary, and perhaps the next attack, will probably revive the commemorative use of the statue.

And the ephemeral will become cyclical.

T-Shirts

August 12, 2016

Distancing oneself and shifting one's viewpoint are among the main driving forces in the sociological gaze. This movement is the source of these chronicles. My three-week long absence from Paris confirms how much the place and position from which we observe something determines what we will see.

In the countryside around Mont Blanc, where I spent my holidays, I tried to break with my position as an observer. My new environment helped me. Conversations rarely covered the attacks and the traces of a relationship with the event were scarcely felt.

Distance from the neighborhood, both social and geographical, helped me once again realize how living there shapes my relation to the events. This distancing is limited, though. My sociological and experiential *habitus* from the year 2015–2016 in the 11th arrondissement in Paris, have apparently led me to develop a hypersensitivity to all signals of any kind of connection with the attacks.

In a nature reserve, a family holiday attraction, for example, I noticed two men each wearing a black t-shirt explicitly referring to "Charlie," not together but in the space of about ten meters squared. The two men were around the same age and were both fathers. One was wearing a t-shirt featuring a circus — an acrobat is juggling balls each bearing one letter of the word "Charlie" — using irony and light-heartedness to evoke the event. The second t-shirt contained only text. Instead of the slogan "Je suis Charlie," of which it imitated the font and format, it proclaimed "Je suis Charlie Martel." This is a reference to Charles Martel's victory over the Muslim conquest

▲ Photographs taken at 4.30 pm on August 12, 2016.

of Poitiers in 732, and it is a formulation used by extreme-right groups like *Génération Identiaire.*[1]

To me, these t-shirts were the most banal material manifestation of the political rift that now runs through French society, torn as to what lessons to take from the attacks. This experience also shows to what extent the most ordinary public space has become a space for the expression of these political struggles that can no longer be reduced to one or several specific arenas.

1 *Generation identitaire* is an extreme-right political group, mostly attracting young people around the themes of defending cultural identity, anti-immigration, and anti-Islam.

Cycle

September 1, 2016

▲ New flags, Boulevard Voltaire, August 29, 2016. The one on the building opposite was taken down over the summer.

The events that occurred over the summer have confirmed that the very term "event" — which was even used for the title of the first of these chronicles — may not be entirely appropriate. Must we now think about this on a new level? Is it even possible to think in terms of chronological milestones (Boucheron & Riboulet, 2015)? And, furthermore, must we now question the very possibility of a collective temporality?

Yesterday, the day before school went back, the residents of my neighborhood were able to take stock of just how impossible it is to find closure after the "event" of November 13. The holiday break had almost made them forget the police presence. Yet, on August 31, the streets where our children go to school were once again blocked off and heavily guarded. Apparently unaware (or uncaring?) of the fear that the parents in the neighborhood had felt and had to overcome throughout 2015,[1] the Ministries of National Education and the Interior had chosen our local school as the site for a speech on the security of school buildings. This speech, and the police protection that accompanied the ministers' presence, provoked renewed anxiety and again attracted deeply unwelcome attention to our neighborhood. Most of all, it gave use the feeling of an endlessly recurring event.

It has become clear in many ways that it is impossible to reduce the temporality of things to a beginning, a middle, and an end — or even simply to a before and an after.

During the month of August, new French flags appeared in the windows, while others were taken down. Sometimes they were put up for a day and then disappeared... and then even (occasionally) reappeared. The entry into a new era thus seems to be accompanied by a breakdown in temporalities: everyone hangs their flag at their own rhythm and according to their own timeframe, even though the act is clearly part of a social dynamic, which still needs to be studied and understood.

---

1 The children's school is situated exactly halfway between the Bataclan and the former offices of *Charlie Hebdo,* where the shooting took place. *See Map.*

∧ Photographs taken
August 26 and 29, 2016.

Today on the Place de la République, only the Memory Oak remains as a reminder of the memorial that once covered the base of the statue. The tree has now been reinvested by the members of the group 17 *Never again* who have put their logo up there. And sometimes passersby stop to look at it.

Although the south side of the base of the statue remains clear of all messages, it continues to be visited and photographed as a "memorial," as though its function remains. It is as though it is waiting to be revived by tributes for the next attack, once again in a kind of cycle.

It is now no longer a question of how to live "after," but how to live "with." Just like with other events and situations, both public and private, which have happened since or which were there before November 13, 2015. As for me, this new temporality implies a return to a form of analysis that is written in the long term, once again dissociating the resident from the sociologist.

⌃ Photographs taken on
   August 27 and 28, 2016.

Heritage

September 20, 2016

The abundance of messages, drawings and tributes that blossomed in the streets of my neighborhood after the attacks was one of the reasons I began these chronicles. Although the graffiti, street art and tributes will probably return to take possession of the streets of this part of the 11th arrondissement, for the moment they are gone. Some tributes were destroyed or thrown away, others were stolen. Many were collected by the Paris Archives.

Last weekend, September 17 and 18, was the 33rd edition of European Heritage Day, and this year the theme was "Heritage and Citizenship." To mark this occasion, the Paris Archives proposed an exhibition in the 19th arrondissement, entitled "The Case of the Tributes to the Victims of the November 13, 2015 Attacks, collected in January 2016: from the Street to the Archives." Writing this final chronicle thus took me out of my neighborhood, and the 11th arrondissement.

The act of archiving means stating what should be remembered from the past and declared to be heritage, and choosing the words that should be used to do this. These "things" left in the street, in the public space, which these chronicles have constantly referred to in fluctuating terms, must now only be considered as "tributes." Much could be said about the few that were chosen to be on display in the Archives that day, and about the professional and institutional constraints that were behind this selection. There was clearly a selection in favor of the most graphic and the most colorful documents, giving priority to consensual messages, those expressing patriotic sentiment and cultural references. There was also an emphasis on the letters, drawings and objects left by children, these famous "future generations," who are naturally the target of all heritage and memory policy, both in France and elsewhere.

⌃ Along with these display cases, there was also a slideshow lasting more than an hour, in the adjacent auditorium.

▲ "Jar of sorrows", made by students from an 11th arrondissement primary school

But it was firstly with the intention of observing and even interviewing some of the visitors, that I went to the exhibition on that Sunday afternoon. European Heritage Day was a great success for the Archives[1] this year, attracting many more visitors than last year, even though its opening hours were shorter (only two afternoons as opposed to two whole days last year). It is clear that most of the visitors to the Archives had come to see the exhibition of tributes rather than the Archives themselves. Although they were invited to join a guided tour of the buildings when they arrived, nearly a third of them visited only the exhibition.

These visitors, so numerous this year, also seemed different from those ordinarily seen at the Archives: both in the fact that they were not local to the 19th and 20th arrondissements where the Archives are, but also

1   Many thanks to Guillaume Nahon, the director of the Paris Archives and his teams, for their warm welcome and support.

because they were young, even very young, with a third of the visitors under 25 years old. Although these Heritage Days were a success for the Archives, they also seem to provide a sketch of the public that feels the most concerned by these tributes, or at least those concerned by the fact that they have been put in a museum. Nearly a year of field observation on the sites of the attacks in the 11th arrondissement suggest that those who came to the Archives on this weekend were on average younger than those observed at the grassroots memorials, which have now disappeared.

I spoke at length with a woman aged 45. She attracted my attention because she looked very closely at each display case, and watched the whole slideshow, and spoke for a long time with the staff of the archives about the collection, and the plan to digitalize it and put it online. As it happened, she was a former resident of the 11th arrondissement, who had now lived in Strasburg for some years. On the one hand, the visit to the exhibition seemed to be a way for her to connect with the events that she did not experience in Paris, and on the other, to participate in a moment that she described on several occasions as "historic." She comes to Paris once a month for a long weekend, and returned to the sites of the attacks, each time just a few weeks after they took place.

"But for *Charlie Hebdo* it was too late, there was nothing left. No messages, or flowers. I couldn't even go past, I was too afraid of breaking down." But she never left anything herself. "Frankly, it never occurred to me. But today, it is not as hard to come as I thought it would be. It's the last piece of the puzzle in a way. And I'm happy to see so many young people. Because what we are living through, it's historic; it will be a part of the history books for children. Of course. All these documents. It's for posterity, it's for memory. When we look at what the Second World War was, it's important to have documents and testimonies. This is the same, this heritage, it's for future generations."

The visit to the tributes on display enables people to participate in history, almost vicariously. The diverse expression of memories has made way for a construction of a more unified and unifying heritage which will — and this is its vocation — progressively construct a cohesive discourse on the attacks and the reactions they provoked.

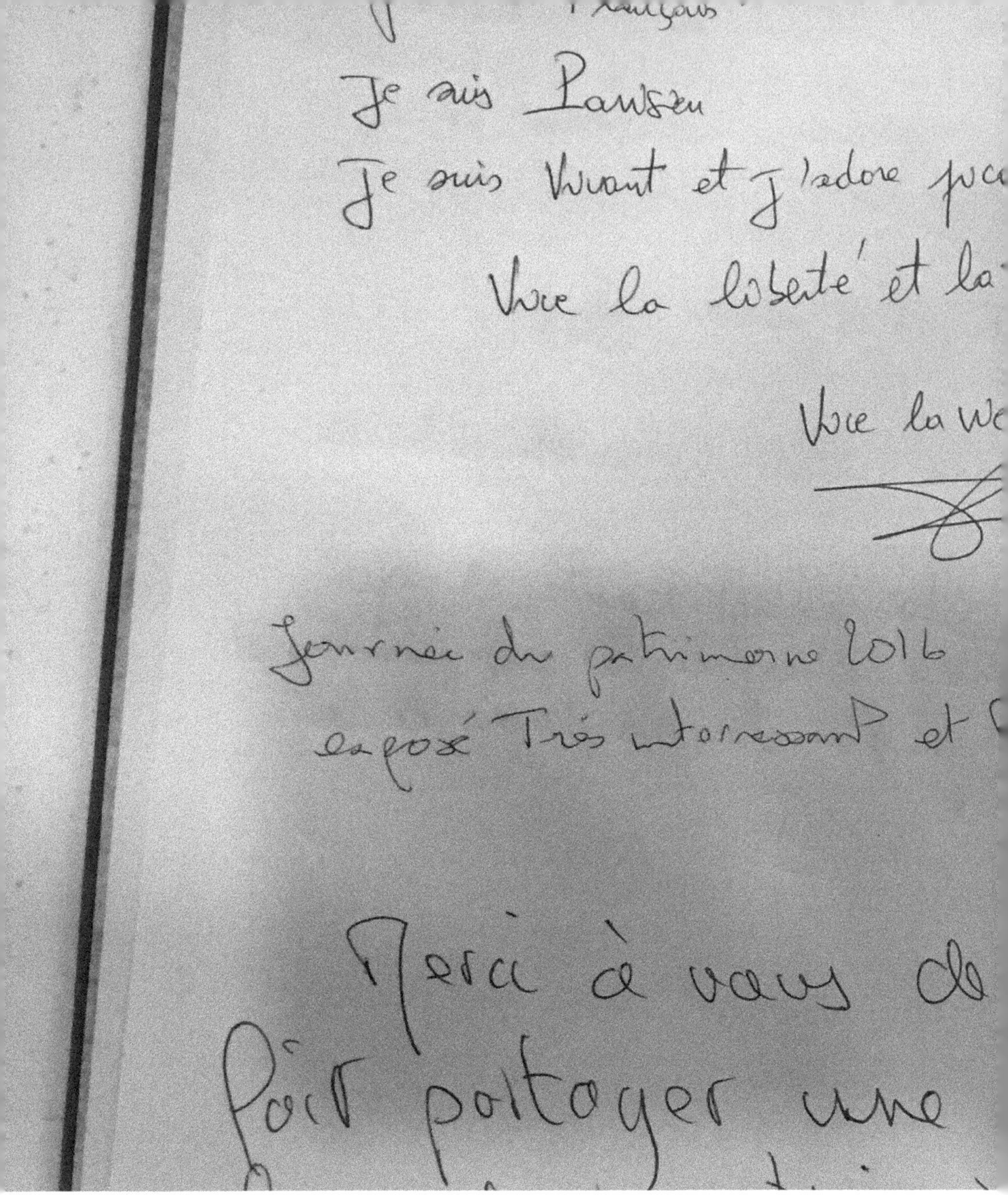

Je suis Lawsen

Je suis Vivant et j'adore pœ

Vive la liberté et la

Vive la W

Journée du patrimoine 2016

exposé Très intéressant et

Merci à vous de

Pour partager une

This heritagization and the legitimation effects that it necessarily produces
— for the victims, for some of the authors of the tributes, for the visitors, for
the Archives apparently, as well as for researchers (including myself), and
many others — clearly constitute a fascinating subject for further research

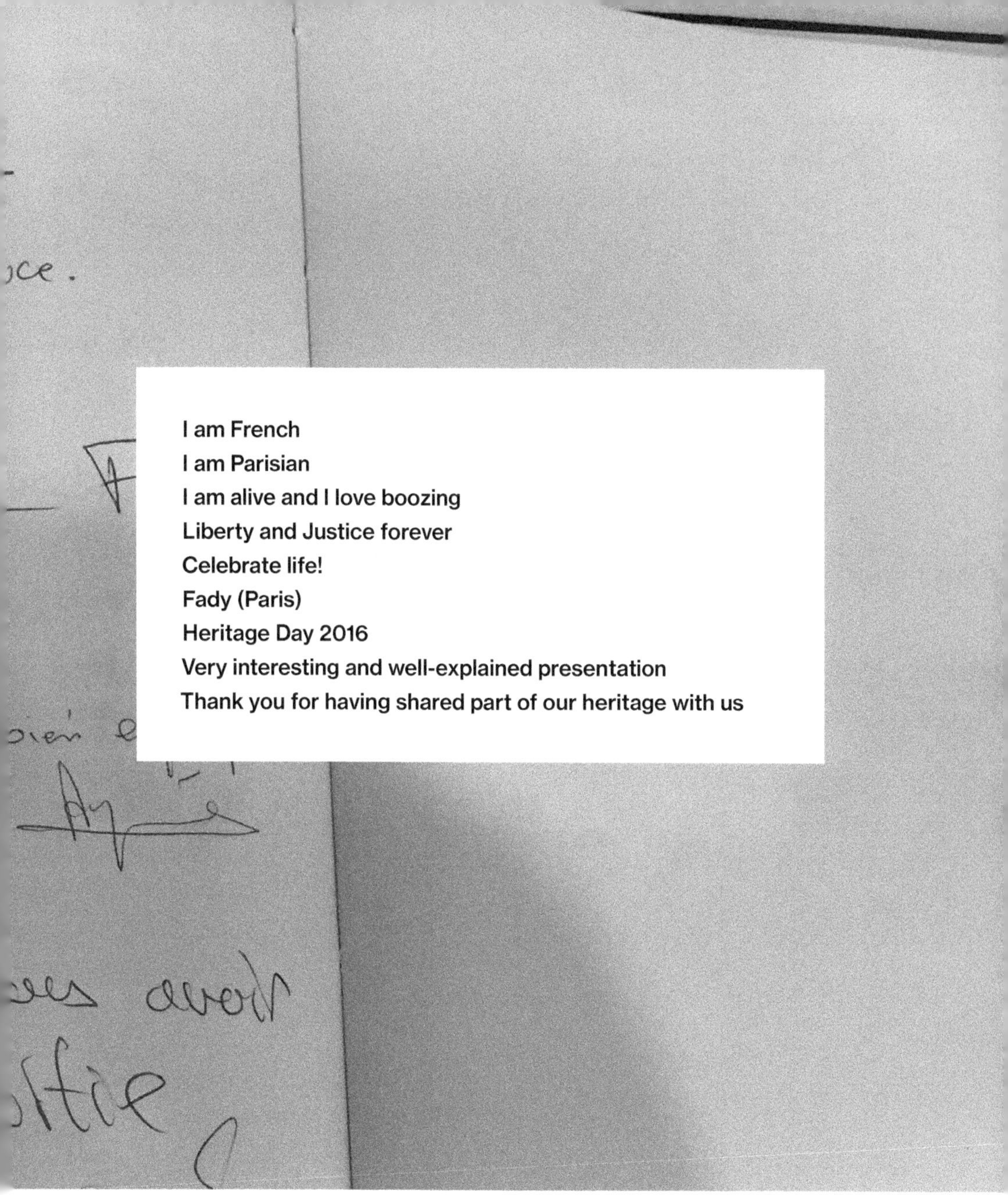

I am French
I am Parisian
I am alive and I love boozing
Liberty and Justice forever
Celebrate life!
Fady (Paris)
Heritage Day 2016
Very interesting and well-explained presentation
Thank you for having shared part of our heritage with us

and analysis. The urban traces that bore the memory of the 2015 attack, and which have been the subject of these chronicles, have been moved from the street to the museum. This shift therefore marks the end of these chronicles, but also the beginning of a new and different story.

Conclusion

An Unfinished Memorialization:
Archives, Monuments and Museums

Since the last chronicle, the legacy of these grassroots memorials has continued, despite the fact that they were initially destined to be ephemeral. Back in July 2016, the French government created a "national medal for the recognition of victims of terrorism." The material form of this medal set the grassroots memorial of the Place de la République into stone. "The front [of the medal] resembles a flower with five petals, marked with white stripes, to evoke the color of the ribbon, with five olive leaves to symbolize the value of peace within the Republic. The center is edged with a blue band bearing the inscription 'République Française,' and on the silver circle at the center is a representation of the statue of the Place de la République." [1] Here the very localization of the grassroots memorials is set in metal.

Over the course of 2017 and 2018, several collections of documents were added to the Paris Archives. As Peter J. Margy and Cristina Sanchez-Carretoro put it, "there is a trend in western societies to preserve the materiality of these [grassroots] memorials" (2011, p. 16). Some members of the Association *17 Never Again* who, as we saw, appointed themselves guardians of this ephemeral memorial, contacted the director of the archives to resolve the conflict that had pitted them against the town Council between January 2015 and August 2016. These memory actors eventually entrusted the documents and images that they had progressively taken home from the monument to the care of the municipal archives. Similarly, the editorial staff of Charlie Hebdo received hundreds of letters after the shootings in their

---

1   Created by decree n°2016-949 of July 16, 2016, "On the creation of the national medal for recognition of victims of terrorism". This medal can only be awarded in relation to events occurring after January 1, 2006.

offices and over the course of 2018, these were also passed on to the Paris Archives. The Archives have thus emerged as a significant actor in the ongoing construction of the heritage around the immediate memorialization of the attacks.

By now readers will know that these collections are by no means spontaneous, nor exhaustive (Yaeger, 2003). As the days passed, these "memory assemblages" (Santino, 1986), these things left in the street, were subject to weather damage, theft, and regular "sorting" by the memorial's self-proclaimed guardians. "The self-censorship of racist messages deposited within tributes to victims occurs at all post-terrorist memorials — curators erase and alter texts which do not express an attitude of tolerance and unity. People produce an image of social unity and 'standing' together after attacks, when the reality is more complex" (Heath-Kelly, 2017). The work of collecting these tributes, was itself subject to specific protocols. It resulted in the destruction of several elements, including many flags considered "redundant" because repetitive (Gazette des archives, 2018). Finally, the additional documents left by many individuals, of which these examples are by no means exhaustive, ultimately resulted in a frozen snapshot of the heritage process around ephemeral memorial, which reflects a thick topography of the memory of the 2015 terrorist attacks in Paris. The archival collections now cover, in decreasing order of quantity, the tributes left around the Bataclan, those from the cafés, and finally, but to a lesser extent, the memorial from the Place de la République, completed by the letters from the Charlie Hebdo paper.

In contrast, the construction of this heritage does not concern the immediate memorialization of the killing of a policewoman in Montrouge on January 8, 2015, or the shooting in the Hyper Casher supermarket in the east of Paris, on the edges of the towns Saint-Mandé and Vincennes, where on January 9, 2015, a gunman held shoppers hostage, leaving four people dead and two wounded, among the practicing Jews who were the store's primary clientele. It also does not concern the terrorist attack of November 13, 2015 around the Stade de France in Saint-Denis, which left one person dead and several seriously injured.[2] In this respect, the ongoing construction of

2   The population of Saint-Denis was also marked by the massive and spectacular police action in the neighborhood on November 18, after the attacks, as they pursued and arrested some of those involved in organizing the attacks.

heritage produces as much forgetting and silence as it does memory. These events on the social and geographical margins also led to marginalization in terms of heritage and memory. The 10th and 11th districts of Paris are at the very heart of the city. Saint-Denis, Montrouge, Saint-Mandé and Vincennes are all on its very edges. Similarly, each of these three events was conceptualized by the authorities as targeting so-called "specific" groups: Jews, the police, and, in the case of Saint-Denis, a geographic area frequently associated with high immigration and minority ethno-religious groups.

The scale at which the fieldwork for this book was conducted *de facto* contributes to this memorial marginalization. Indeed, my decision to work "on my doorstep," by definition, limited the perimeter of study. As in other respects, hopefully it will be completed by other studies conducted from other positions and perspectives on the memorialization of the attacks. We must therefore question the social and symbolic stratification that is produced by the construction of heritage, even when it concerns a traumatic event considered as vehicling collective resilience. This conclusion forces us to pay attention to the dynamics of social exclusion and marginalization that are associated with all constructions of collective memory.[3]

For the moment, the social uses of this heritage, previously unprecedented in France,[4] are yet to be explored. Most likely they will be situated somewhere between performance and archives, as Diana Taylor has suggested in relation to other fieldsites (Taylor, 2003; Ekström, 2012). We can already see how they make it impossible to distinguish between a "pre-memorial era" (Simpson and Corbridge, 2006) and a subsequent "era of commemoration" (Nora, 1997). The immediate reactions to the attacks on one hand, and the commemoration of the events on the other, is necessarily a continuum. These are stages in the ongoing process of memorialization. They

---

3   This marginalization also takes place on the global level. Several researchers commented on the difference in reactions following the attacks in Beirut on November 12 and in Paris on November 13, 2015, although Islamic State claimed responsibility for both (Jouan, 2017).

4   Although such archival collection was unprecedented, this is not true for the construction of grassroots memorials or collective assemblies, which were observed in Paris as early as the 19th century (Salomé, 2010) and which have occurred more regularly since the 20th century (Salomé, 2015).

demonstrate, if indeed it was necessary to do so, the "restlessness of events" (Wagner-Pacifici, 2010).

Once again, the precedent of 9/11 has outlined possible scenarios for this articulation between immediate reactions and long-term memorialization, between grassroots memorials and memorial-museums. Today, in the 9/11 Memorial & Museum, visitors are invited to "tell their 9/11" in exchange for a promise that this narrative will be preserved "for the future." Inversely, Marita Sturken has shed light on the fetishization of tributes, which have become heritage, in the museography developed within the memorial museum. "Known as the Last Column, this thirty-six-foot-high steel colossus is covered with messages to the dead, photographs, and memorial inscriptions put there by firefighters, police, rescue workers, and other laborers who worked at the recovery mission at Ground Zero for nine months. [...] As the museum itself narrates, 'Standing tall once again, the Last Column will encourage reflection on the foundations of resilience, hope, and community with which we might build our collective future'" (Sturken, 2015, p. 471).

In Spain, the messages left in response to the terrorist attacks in Madrid on March 11, 2004, also constitute primary sources for the national commemorative monument (Truc, 2018). Some of them were engraved into the immense glass monument set up on the site of the Atocha train station, which was the epicenter of the attacks. In Brussels too, the town authorities are considering using these "tributes," now preserved in the town archives, to build a future monument, possibly engraving them into the ground on the Place de la Bourse, where most of the gatherings after the attacks of March 22, 2016 were held (Milosevic, 2017 and 2018).

In the French case, the "memorial" destiny of these tributes to the victims of the 2015 attacks has yet to be decided. For the moment, they have been digitized. A website was set up by the Paris Archives in November 2016, allowing people to read them online.[5] In addition to this, and also to mark the first anniversary of the attacks, the Association *Life for Paris,* one of the two support organizations for the victims of November 13, decided to present an exhibition of a selection of tributes in the multipurpose community center of the 11th district, in partnership with the Paris Archives. Similarly, also in November 2016, an artist decided to display photographs of these tributes on

5   http://archives.paris.fr/r/137/hommages-aux-victimes-des-attentats-de-2015/.

walls around neighborhood and directly around the Bataclan to commemorate the first anniversary of the killings.

By the end of June 2018, the Paris Archives' website for consulting the tributes to the victims of the 2015 attacks had been visited more than 100,000 times.[6] This interest from users peaked during the annual commemoration, with 10,485 consultations in November 2017, compared to 3,224 the previous month, and 488 for the following month. For the moment, the construction of the heritage of the events goes hand in hand with their commemoration.

This cyclical temporal framing, the time map as Eviatar Zerubavel put it (2003), is associated with a memorial topography. As I write these lines, three years after the events, several sites in the Parisian public space bear witness to their memory. These sites were all inaugurated during annual commemorations of the events. In reading these chronicles, the reader has already encountered this first round of memory. For the first anniversary of the January 2015 attacks, the Paris's City Council and the French presidency initially considered planting seventeen trees on the Place de la République, one for each victim. This tree-planting was a reference to an established sign of resilience (Zerubavel, 1996; Gensburger, 2016). Trees were already used to represent the memory of the attacks in Madrid (Truc, 2017b), New York (Goldberger, 2005) or in Oklahoma City (Linenthal, 2001).

The organization of the tree-planting was in its advanced stages when the November 13 shootings occurred. Once again, the same neighborhood was in the heart of the attacks. It was quite simply impossible to consider planting a forest of 147 trees in such a small place in the middle of Paris.[7] So it was eventually decided that a single symbolic tree would be planted on the edges of the Place, on the side of the 10th district. At the base of the "Memory Oak," was a plaque bearing the following inscription: "In memory of the victims of the terrorist attacks in January and November 2015 in Paris, Montrouge and Saint-Denis. The French people pay homage to them here." This tree of memory and the plaque that accompanies it commemorate events that were scarcely two months old at the time the tree was inaugurated by the French

---

6 Many thanks to Gaël Donneger and Guillaume Nohon for these figures, which are accurate as of June 26, 2018.

7 For more information about the state's decisions on symbolic politics relating to the attacks, see (Boussaguet & Faucher, 2017a and 2017b).

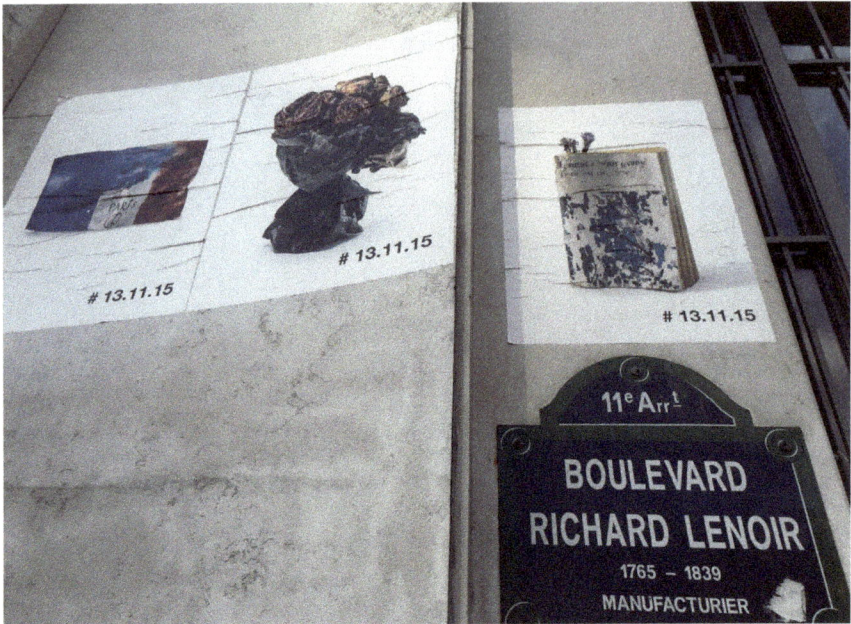

President and the Mayor of Paris in January 2016. This official commemorative monument was erected even as people's spontaneous public expression of memory, particularly through the grassroots memorial, was at its height, only a few dozen meters from the tree, in the center of the Place de la République.

Like an allegory, the first tree got sick and had to be replaced. Since then, it has had to be looked after very carefully. In any event, the tree has never been genuinely appropriated as a site of memory. Regular observation has shown that it is not visited, and most of those who use the Place — both tourists and Parisians — do not even know it exists. Nor has the tree given rise to any political appropriations. During the commemorations of the second and third anniversaries of November 13, no official state representative left a wreath there or made any official gestures of commemoration. In this respect, the social uses of this space are by no means exceptional. Gérôme Truc remarks that, "after November 13, 2015, the attacks in Paris having suddenly revived the memory of those that left Madrid bereaved 11 years earlier, the Spanish media reported that the memorial at the Atocha station was closed to the public for several weeks due to lack of maintenance, which had apparently shocked no one", until then (Truc, 2017b, p. 92).

In Paris, however, the topography of memorialization of the attacks can be distinguished from that of Madrid by its polycentrism. Like in London, the Paris attacks, in January and in November 2015 targeted several places, although some of these were in the same neighborhood. In November 2016, for the first anniversary of the events, after these chronicles were finished, the Paris City Council and the French government made the decision to have the memorial topography reflect the cartography of the attacks. A commemorative plaque was inaugurated in each of the sites affected (cafés, concert hall, and football stadium). The use of this commemorative tool was by no means original. As the reader will have noted in several chronicles that describe the inauguration of such plaques for the first anniversary of the January 2015 attacks, such inauguration is frequent and highly codified by French public authorities. The text on the plaques systematically list the dates and the full names of the victims.

The plaques inaugurated in November 2016 are an exception to this (Antichan, Gensburger & Griveaud, 2017). They do bear the names of all the victims who died in each place, but — unlike the previous ones — they are not fixed to the walls of the buildings in which the killings took place. So as not to interfere with the return to business as usual, they are all several meters away, set on public buildings or on street fixtures. Only the façade of the Bataclan concert hall has a small plaque that refers viewers to the public square across the road where there is the main official commemorative plaque listing the names of the dead.

These sites are torn between mourning the 130 people all killed in a single night,[8] and returning to normal economic activity, particularly for the cafés and concert hall (Heath-Kelly, 2016). It is therefore difficult for commemoration to find its rightful place.

Both the Bonne Bière café and the Bataclan concert hall do not have buildings in front of them upon which a plaque can be set, so public squares were chosen instead. In the first case, the plaques are attached to the iron railings that surround the square. In the second, the commemorative stone is set among the greenery of the square. In both cases, there is a constant tension between a search for visibility and a desire for invisibility, which explains the progressive evolution of these memorials, following demands from survivors and from families who did not want anything to cover or hide the names of their dead.

In addition to their ordinary uses, most often by the families of victims and by tourists, who are indeed a new feature of the neighborhood (Lisle, 2004), these sites of memory also serve to designate a shared space for commemoration, even if they are slightly removed from the sites of the attacks. Each participant is liable to award it a different meaning. But everyone agrees that the annual ceremony to honor the victims should be held there.[9] Each November 13, the survivors and victims' families, individually or as part of victims' associations, return to these sites one after the other. These ceremonies are also attended by the Mayor of Paris, Anne Hildago, and a state representative, the French President, or the Prime Minister — François Hollande in 2016, Emmanuel Macron in 2017, and Eduard Philippe in 2018. They each lay an official wreath in turn, but none speaks. The ceremonies are completely silent (Brown, 2012). There is only the reading of the names of the dead, a now global necronomalist ritual (Laqueur, 2016), to break the silence. This

8   In addition, 7 of the perpetrators were also killed that night.

9   For this occasion, a temporary stone memorial, a replica of the one in the square, was placed outside the concert hall.

∧ The plaque on the facade of the building in two successive versions: in November 2016, and before the third anniversary, in November 2018. It now directs readers to cross the road to see the memorial in the square.

▲ The plaque opposite the Bataclan, in the park, in November 2016, then set on a stone base to protect it from the mud, prior to the third anniversary in November 2018.

litany, alternating feminine and masculine voices, was pre-recorded for the first anniversary and has been replayed every year since.

There are more and more spectators every year who attend these sites to observe the ceremonies. Both before and after the reading of the names and the one minute of silence that follows, they are generally engaged in intense discussion. Their comments are political, for example, critically reflecting on the fact that the president and other ministers remain silent.[10] Ethnographic observation of these ceremonies clearly demonstrates that there is no consensus around the meaning of the attacks and how — and which — memories of them should be preserved. Behind the commemorative consensus that characterizes much of these ephemeral memorials, and beyond the questions around resilience that run through French society as a whole, the multiplicity of meanings given to the attacks and their memory are clearly visible here. They also demonstrate the symbolic weakness of the contemporary political representation on this issue (Boussaguet and Faucher, 2017 a and 2017b).

The polycentrism of the sites and the polysemy of their memorialization are also accompanied by a polymorphic community mobilization. Almost immediately after the night of November 13, two organizations to support victims emerged. They each bring together survivors and families and loved ones of people who were killed. Yet they have significantly different sociological profiles. The members of *Life for Paris* are mostly young, either survivors or loved ones of survivors of the Bataclan. The other organization, *13onze15 Fraternité et Vérité* has older members, who are, for the most part, parents of people who died in cafés or in the Bataclan.[11] For the two first anniversaries of November 13, in 2016 and in 2017, each of these organizations

---

10 These observations were conducted with Sylvain Antichan, Delphine Griveaud and Solveig Hennebert.

11 In France, non-profit organizations, known as "associations", must be registered with the state. *Life for Paris* was registered on January 30, 2016 under official number W751232465, and *13onze15, Fraternité et Vérité*, on January 23, 2016, under official number W751232388. Consulted in December 2018, the database of the official record of associations also shows that since January 7, 2015, more than 20 associations have been created with the objective of perpetuating the memory of the attacks which occurred since.

held their own separate ceremony immediately following the official parade. *Life for Paris* set up on the steps of the town hall of the 11th district and organized a concert and released a balloon for each victim. *13onze15* gathered near the 10th district to light lanterns that were then set off on the Canal Saint Martin, which runs just behind the Place de la République.

However, 2018 marked the beginning of a new era of commemoration, a phase of institutionalization that was based on (sometimes conflictual) collaboration — as always in France — between the different levels of French government. This new period is organized around the question of the erection of a new commemorative monument. This is not in itself new, of course. As mentioned in the chronicles, immediately after the attacks an ad hoc organization named *Generation* Bataclan was created by communication professionals without any direct connection to the events or the places concerned. It intended to design a commemorative monument and raise funds to build it.[12] It rapidly organized a call for projects that was publicized on its website. In parallel to this, as early as 2016, the internationally recognized American artist, Jeff Koons, designed a monument project of a giant hand holding multicolored flowers. He intended to make a gift of this sculpture to the city of Paris, on the condition that the latter raise the funds required to build it.

Initially, these projects met with limited response. But, in the beginning of 2018, the two victims' organizations have suddenly taken a shared position, in public and determined opposition to the two self-appointed actors of memory and their monumental projects, which have been immediately de-legitimized as a result. We can see that, as Rothberg says, "multidirectional exchange takes place beyond the forms of cultural ownership that motivate competitive struggles over the past" (2009: p. 158). Indeed, in 2018, both the French state and the City of Paris had created commissions and working groups to enable the erection of both a national, and also a municipal, monument. These solicitations by these two government bodies had led the two victims' associations to eventually stand together. For the third anniversary, on November 13, 2018, they organized a single shared ceremony that was

12 This association was registered on November 28 2015 under the number W751231695; https://www.generationbataclan.fr.

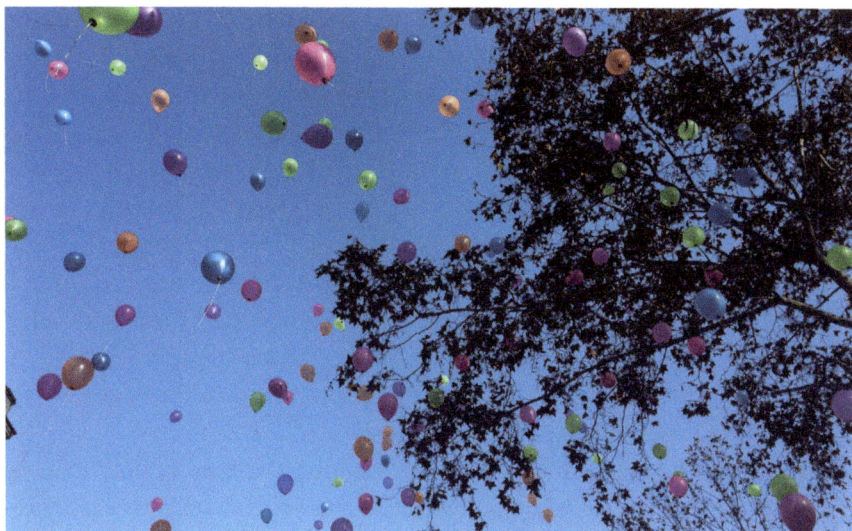

∧ Balloon release, November 13, 2018, outside the City Hall of the 11th district.

held on the steps of the City Hall of the 11th district, where each of the presidents of the organizations spoke.

These two speeches were also the opportunity for each of these victims' organizations to celebrate the state's intention to inaugurate, in Paris, a national museum and memorial for victims of terrorism,[13] despite criticisms from other towns and organizations, such as that of the victims of the Nice attack that occurred on July 14, 2016.

Similarly, the City of Paris's proposal to construct a monument in the urban space contributed to these organizations coming together, and helped them move away from the time of mourning and into the time of official commemoration. As was the case for 9/11, the representatives of victims have found themselves in a key role in this new phase of institutionalization of memory, whether it takes the form of a monument or a museum (Levitt, 2011).

Once again, this institutionalization has not been purely consensual. The discussions around the Parisian monument project shed light on the

13 Memory Committee Report, submitted to the Minister of Justice on September 7, 2018, *Terrorisme: Faire face. Enjeux historiques et mémoriaux*, remis à http://www.memoire13novembre.fr/sites/default/files/Terrorisme_Faire_face.pdf.

diversity of victims' experiences.[14] How can a monument "to the victims of the November 13, 2015 terrorist attacks in Paris" be constructed when these people generally have different relationships with the event? Families who have lost loved ones naturally turn toward the idea of setting up a grand funerary monument in the garden of the Père Lachaise cemetery in Paris, a cemetery which is home to many other sites honoring the memory of historic crimes, including those of terrorist attacks against French people since 1980. Their focus is on remembering the dead. But the survivors who were there on the night of November 13 want a monument that celebrates their survival and the collective solidarity that has allowed them to keep going. They consider the "neighborhood of the attack" and the urban space as the only site where such a monument could be created.

After the London bombings, there were similar discussions about where to establish an official monument, in addition to commemorative plaques. The monument was eventually set up in Hyde Park at some distance from the site of the attacks (Matthew & Brown, 2016). However, for several years a neighborhood group continued to demand the construction of another monument in Tavistock Square, the site of one of the attacks, where the only emblematic above-ground photo of the events — the wreckage of a red bus — had been taken. Moreover, this particular London square already had a tree planted in remembrance of Hiroshima and a statue of Ghandi, which for the promoters of the project was in keeping with their political reading of the attacks (Truc, 2012). This additional monument was finally unveiled in September 2018.[15] It is most likely that in Paris too, several monuments will eventually be constructed, given that there are as many different experiences of these events as there are political readings of it; today by non-government actors, tomorrow by those visiting the specific monuments and other museums and memorials (Gensburger, 2020; Huyssen, 2003, Young, 2000).

In June 2018, for example, there was a controversy surrounding the planned performance of the rapper Médine at the Bataclan concert hall, because he was accused of promoting Jihad in some of his texts. *Life for Paris*

---

14 The associations thus asked me to give them information about the ways in which other traumatic events and collective mourning had given rise to monuments in the Paris city space.

15 https://www.bbc.com/news/uk-england-london-45485154.

refused to comment on the controversy but *13onze15* expressed their desire that the performance be held elsewhere. An extreme-right group used this as an opportunity to make the public space into a monument by putting portraits of the victims on the walls of the concert hall and pretending to take stand on their behalf.

There are already several sites of memory that bear witness to the 2015 terrorist attacks in Paris, but this polycentrism can also be seen in the calendar of the events. Along with the plaques, national days of remembrance are the other traditional tool for public commemoration in France (Gensburger, 2014). In the American case, the 2001 attacks all happened on one day. It was therefore immediately clear, as early as October 2001, that the single date of September 11 would be chosen by the President George Bush, upon recommendation from the US House of Representatives, as the date for Patriot Day. The question of an official date for the commemoration of the 2015 Paris attacks was more complicated. The events took place within a history of terrorism that, in the French context, began well before 2015 and unfortunately has continued after. For example, since 2001, the organization *SOS Attentats* (SOS Attacks), which has since become the French Association for Victims of Terrorism (Association française des Victimes du Terrorisme (AfVT)), has held a "national homage to victims of terrorism" each year on September 19. This date was originally chosen because it was the day when, in 1989, 170 people were killed in the attack on UTA flight 722, a former French airline. Although this annual ceremony on September 19 was instigated and organized by a non-government organization, since 2015 it has been systematically attended by state representatives. Consequently, on September 19, 2018, the French President Emmanuel Macron announced that he had decided to create a museum and memorial to victims of terrorism in Paris, along with the imminent creation of a national day for this commemoration for the victims of the attacks. But he left the choice of date open: September 19 (1989), January 7 (2015), November 13 (2015), or July 14 (2016), the date of the attack in Nice. Given the significant divergences between victims' associations, the government report behind the original project for the Museum-Memorial suggested opting for the European level — as though rising above the fray — and choosing March 11 as the date, in reference to the European day for the commemoration of victims of terrorism, decided by the European Parliament following the Madrid attacks in 2004. Here the construction of collective memory would involve the adoption of a reference above and beyond the nation, despite the fact that the latter was the primary frame for the events being commemorated.

Reference to overseas examples and the influence of transnational dynamics in commemoration have indeed been characteristic of the memorialization of the 2015 Paris attacks, from the very beginning. To implement and organize the collection of data, the Paris Archives relied on precedents from overseas (Gardner & Henry, 2002), from the New York case to the "Our Marathon" project run by Northeastern University following the Boston attacks in April 2013,[16] as well as the "Charlie archive" initiative at Harvard University[17] that followed the January 2015 attacks in Paris (Green, Huziel & Hollis, 2018). Since then, the Parisian example has in turn, encouraged other initiatives, like those of the Brussels archives in March 2015 (Bazin & Van Eeckenrode, 2018). International guidelines for good practice in this area have also been written (Morin, 2015).

Similarly, as we have seen, the decision to plant a memory tree on the Place de la République, in January 2016, was explicitly linked by political leaders at both the national and local level, to the precedent in Madrid (Boussaguet & Faucher, 2017 a and 2017b). Two months after March 11, 2004, 192 cypress and olive trees were planted across from the Atocha station in Madrid, before being transplanted to Retiro Park. Finally, the Museum-Memorial Project promoted by the French state since September 2018 makes continual reference to the precedent of the 9/11 National Memorial & Museum. The authors of the report behind the project spoke at length to Cliff Chanin, the Executive Vice President and Deputy Director for Museum Programs in the New York institution, and made it clear that his comments were crucial for them.

However, several researchers have emphasized the limits of such comparisons and borrowings (Huyssen, 2009; Young, 2016). Although almost all the actors of memorialization around the events of November 13, 2015 have continually turned toward the New York precedent, the Parisian case is different in several respects. Firstly, where 9/11 led to a massive destruction of buildings and the urban environment, the 2015 Paris attacks had almost no visible consequence in the public space. As a result, the potential projects for

16 https://marathon.library.northeastern.edu/.

17 http://cahl.io.

monuments, museums, and memorials are both less indispensable and more open in the French case. The temporality of the events is also profoundly different. September 11, 2001 has in many ways remained an isolated event in American history. From a short-term perspective, November 13, 2015 came after the events of January 7 and 9 of the same year, and was followed by several other terrorist attacks, including the devastating attack in Nice that left eighty-six people dead, including thirteen children. The continuity in which November 13 took place probably explains why the French flags put up in autumn 2015 remained in place much longer than the nine months of those studied by the American sociologist, Randall Collins, in 2001 (2004). Many of them are in fact still in the windows as I write these lines, three years later. Several studies have shown the differential social effects of a one-time attack and chronic terrorism (Spilerman and Stecklov, 2009).

Moreover, from a long-term perspective, the city of Paris and its inhabitants have confronted many traumatic events — from the waves of terrorism, in the 1980s and 90s, to the Second World War and the German occupation –that is likely to build a specific attitude toward adversity among residents. The specificity of this experience still needs to be studied in detail. This should be elucidated by the collection of testimonies and life histories such as those conducted by the "November 13" research program (Eustache & Peschanski, 2016). Several studies have already demonstrated that the London attacks in 2005 were read and remembered by many Londoners through the memory of the Blitz, the massive bombing of the British capital by German planes during the Second World War (Jackson & Hall, 2016). Other works have advocated a socio-history of the social reactions to terrorist attacks (Silke, 2007; Siman-Tov, Bodas & Peleg, 2016). In this respect, fluctuating as it does between memory and forgetting, between immediacy and the long term, the memorialization of the 2015 terrorist attacks in Paris is still ongoing.

Paris, Boulevard Voltaire, December 11, 2018

Acknowledgement

As the reader now knows, my partner Renaud, and our children, Norah and Jacob, have often wandered the streets of our neighborhood with me. It is thus also through their eyes that I have seen the city, and sometimes with their words that I have described it.

Thanks, as always, to them for their love, their curiosity, and their patience.

This book owes much to discussions that I regularly had with shopkeepers, neighbors and friends in the area, and particularly with the parents at my children's schools, but also with visitors passing through, whether Parisians or tourists. I hope that, each in their own way, they find here an understanding of the place in which they live, and which they come to visit.

Particular thanks to Danièle Rousselier, my friend and neighbor, for her constant encouragement. Also to Isabelle Backouche, my friend and colleague, a specialist of the history of Paris, so closely touched by the events of November 13.

These chronicles are also part of a collective approach to research. My thanks firstly to Sylvain Antichan, Maëlle Bazin, Brian Chauvel, Sandrine Clérisse but also to Micol Bez, Marion Charpenel, Hélène Frouard, Brett Le Saint, Cécile Rodrigues and Jeanne Teboul. A special thanks to Gérôme Truc who constantly encouraged me in the translation process of the French version of this book and in the writing of the two additional introductive and conclusive chapters.

Several people, Omar, Driss and Sabine, helped me with their linguistic skills. And my sister Clara for her help in graphic designing.

I would like to thank my colleagues at the Institut des Sciences sociales du Politique for their support and their benevolence toward this form of writing: Sophie Duchesne, Alexandre Jaunait, Marie-Claire Lavabre, Sandrine Lefranc, Aleksandra Mikanovic, Jérôme Tournadre, and Magali Vautelin. Indeed, these texts were first published, in French, between December 2015 and September 2016 in the blog *Sociology on my Doorstep: Chronicles of the "Bataclan" neighborhood,* a form of expression that is still unusual and iconoclastic among researchers in France.

Finally, I would like to thank Andrew Hoskins, Matthew Allen and Scott Straus for their reviews and advice in the preparation of an English and revised version of this book. I am also very grateful to Mirjam Truwant and Leuven University Press for their trust and of course to Katharine Throssell, who translated this book. I am very lucky to be able to count on such a partner in writing.

Since the initial publication of the first version of this book in France, I have had the privilege to meet and talk with some of the November 13 victims' organizations who were looking for clues. I hope that this book, and especially its conclusions, may help them to move forward with their questions, doubts and commemorative projects.

References

Alexander, J. C. (2012). *Trauma: A Social Theory*. Cambridge, UK: Polity Press.

Allen, M. (2015). *The Labour of Memory. Memorial Culture and 7/7*. Basingstoke, UK: Palgrave Macmillan.

Allen, M., & Brown. S.D. (2016). Memorial meshwork: The making of the commemorative space of the Hyde Park 7/7 Memorial. *Organization, 23*(1), 10–28.

Allerton, C. (ed.) (2016). *Children: Ethnographic Encounters*. London, UK: Bloomsbury Publishing.

Antichan, S. (2014). Mettre la France en tableaux. La formation politique et sociale d'une iconographie nationale au musée historique du château de Versailles (1830–1950). *Political Science dissertation, advisor Yves Deloye*, Paris, France: Université Paris-1.

Antichan, S. (2016). Comment étudier les pratiques mémorielles liées aux attentats ? Plaidoyer pour des sciences sociales ordinaires. *Genèses, 4*(109), 139–156.

Antichan, S. (2016). S'émouvoir pour Versailles ou l'intimité civique du patrimoine national. Analyse des courriers reçus par le château suite à l'attentat de 1978. *Rapport remis au Centre de Recherches du Château de Versailles*.

Antichan, S., Gensburger, S., & Griveaud, D. (2017). La mémoire en ses lieux. Essai de topographie de la première commémoration du 13 novembre 2015 à Paris. *Mémoires en jeu, 4*, 50–59.

Azouvi, F. (2012), *Le mythe du grand silence: Auschwitz, les Français, la mémoire*. Paris, France: Fayard.

Barton, B. (2011). My Auto-Ethnographic Dilemma: Who Owns the Story? *Qualitative Sociology, 34*, 431–445.

Baussant M., & al. (2017). *Les Terrains de la mémoire. Approches croisées à l'échelle locale*. Nanterre, France: Presses de l'Université Paris Ouest, 2017.

Baussant, M. (2002). *Pieds-noirs. Mémoires d'exils*. Paris, France: Stock.

Bazin, M., & Van Eeckenrode, M. (2018). Mise en archives des réactions post-attentats: enjeux et perspectives. *La Gazette des Archives, 250*(2), 9–26.

Bazin, M., & Truc, G. (2019). Les gardiens de la mémoire: mobilisations et conflits d'appropriation autour de mémoriaux post-attentats à Madrid, Londres et Paris. *Ethnologie française*, to be published.

Bertheleu, H. (2014). *Au nom de la mémoire. Le patrimoine des migrations en région Centre*. Paris, France: Presses universitaires François Rabelais.

Bond, L. (2015). *Frames of Memory after 9/11. Culture, Criticism, Politics and Law*. Basingstoke, UK: Palgrave Macmillan.

Boucheron, P., & Riboulet, M. (2015). *Prendre dates. Paris, 6 janvier-14 janvier 2015*. Paris, France: Verdier.

Boussaguet, L., & Faucher, F. (2017a). Quand l'État convoque la rue. La marche républicaine du 11 janvier 2015. *Gouvernement et action publique*, 2(2), 37–61.

Boussaguet, L., & Faucher, F. (2017b). The Politics of Symbols: Reflections on the French Government's Framing of the 2015 Terrorist Attacks. *Parliamentary Affairs*.

Brenner, P. S., & al. (2015). Safety and Solidarity After the Boston Marathon Bombing: A Comparison of Three Diverse Boston Neighborhoods. *Sociological Forum*, 30(1), 40–61.

Brossat, A. (2010). Le cimetière comme hétérotopie. *Appareil* [online], put on-line on September 29 2010, http://appareil.revues.org/1070.

Brice, C. (2008). Monuments: pacificateurs ou agitateurs de mémoire. In P. Blanchard & I. Veyrat-Masson (Eds.), *Les Guerres de mémoires. La France et son histoire* (pp. 199–208), Paris, France: La Découverte.

Brossat, A. (2010). Le cimetière comme hétérotopie. *Appareil*. Retrieved from http://appareil.revues.org/1070.

Brouard, S., Vasilopoulos, P., & Foucault, M. (2018). How terrorism affects political attitudes: France in the aftermath of the 2015–2016 attacks. *West European Politics*, 0(0), 1-27.

Brown, S. D. (2012). Two minutes of silence: social technologies of public commemoration. *Theory & Psychology*, 22(2), 234–252.

Brown, S.D., & Hoskins, A. (2010). Terrorism in the new memory ecology: Mediating and remembering the 2005 London Bombings. *Behavioral Sciences of Terrorism and Political Aggression*, 2, 87–107.

Browning, C. (2006). *Des hommes ordinaires, Le 101e bataillon de réserve de la police allemande et la Solution finale en Pologne*. Paris, France: Les Belles Lettres.

Browning, C. (2018). « Je suis en terrasse »: Political Violence, Civilization Politics, and the Everyday Courage to Be. *Political Psychology*, 39(2), 243–261.

Bertin-Mahieux, C. (2017). Instant History of 9/11. *Mémoire en jeu*, 4, 88–89.

Cesarani, D., & Sundquist, E. J. (2011). After the Holocaust. Challenging the Myth of Silence. In M. M. Clark, P. Bearman, C. Ellis, & S. D. Smith (Eds), *After the fall: New Yorkers remember September 2001 and the years that followed.* New York, NY: The New Press.

Collins, R. (2004). Rituals of solidarity and security in the wake of terrorist attack. *Sociological Theory, 22*(1), 53–87.

Connerton, P. (2008). Seven types of forgetting. *Memory Studies, 1*(1), 59–71.

Culture et Musées. (2013). La muséologie: 20 ans de recherches. juillet-décembre.

Delamont, S. (2009). The only honest thing: autoethnography, reflexivity and small crises fieldwork. *Ethnography and Education, 4*(1), 51–63.

Diner, H. R. (2009). *We Remember with Reverence and Love. American Jews and the Myth of Silence after the Holocaust, 1945–1962.* New York-London, NY-UK: New York University Press.

Doss, E. (2008). *The Emotional Life of Contemporary Public Memorials. Towards a theory of temporary memorials.* Amsterdam, Netherlands: Amsterdam University Press.

Doss, E. (2010). *Memorial Mania: Public Feeling in America.* Chicago, Ill: University of Chicago Press.

Draaisma, D. (2015). *Forgetting. Myths, Perils and Compensations.* New Haven, Conn: Yale University Press.

Drozdzewski, D., & Robinson, D. F. (2015). Care-work on fieldwork: taking your own children into the field. *Children's Geographies, 13*(3), 372–378.

Duckworth, C. L. (2014). *9/11 and Collective Memory in US Classrooms: Teaching About Terror* (1st ed.). New York, NY: Routledge. 146.

Durkheim, E. (1951 [1897]). *Suicide: a study in sociology, The Free Press*

Dyregrov, A., Straume, M., Dyregrov, A., & Gronvold Bugge R. (2016). Weekend gatherings for bereaved family members after the terror killings in Norway in 2011. *Bereavement Care, 35*(1), 22–30.

Edkins, J. (2003). *Trauma and the Memory of Politics.* Cambridge, UK: Cambridge University Press.

Eidelman, J., & al. (2008). *La Place des publics. De l'usage des études et recherches par les musées,* Paris, France: La Documentation française.

Ekström, A. (2012). Exhibiting Disasters: Mediation, Historicity and Spectatorship. *Media, Culture & Society, 34*(4), 472–487.

Ellis, C. (2002). Shattered Lives: Making sense of September 11th and its Aftermath. *Journal of contemporary Ethnography, 31*(4), 375–410.

Erikson, K. (1994). *A new Species of Trouble: explorations in disaster, trauma and community*. New York, NY: W.W. Norton & Co.

Ettorre, E. (2016). *Autoethnography as feminist method: Sensitising the feminist 'I'*. Oxford, UK: Routledge.

Fassin, D. (2010). *La Raison humanitaire. Une histoire morale du temps présent*. Paris, France: Gallimard/Seuil.

Feldman, J.D. (2003). On tragedy in reference to Another: September 11 and the Oblogations of Museum Commemoration. *American Anthropologist, 105*(4), 839–843.

Foner, N. (Ed.) (2005). *Wounded City. The Social Impact of 9/11*. New York, NY: Russel Sage Foundation.

Foucault, M. (2016). Une France trop résiliente ? *Baromètre de la confiance politique — Vague 7*, CEVIPOF.

Fraenkel, B. (2002). *Les Écrits de septembre, New York 2001*. Paris, France: Textuel.

Gardner, J. (2011). September 11: Museums, Spontaneous Memorials and History. In P. Margry & C. Sanchez-Carretero (Eds.), *Grassroots Memorials. The Politics of Memorializing Traumatic Death* (pp. 285–303). New York, NY: Berghahn Books.

Gardner, J. B., & Henry S. M. (2002). September 11 and the Mourning After: Reflections on Collecting and Interpreting the History of Tragedy. *The Public Historian, 24*(3), 37–52.

Gensburger, S. (2014). Comprendre la multiplication des "journées de commémoration nationale": étude d'un instrument d'action publique de nature symbolique. In C. Halpern & al. (Eds.), *L'Instrumentation de l'action publique. Controverses, résistances, effets* (pp. 345–365), Paris, France: Presses de Sciences Po.

Gensburger, S. (2016). *National Policy, Global Memory. The Commemoration of the Righteous among the Nations from Jerusalem to Paris*. New York, NY: Berghahn Books.

Gensburger, S. (2017). *Mémoire vive: Chroniques d'un quartier. Bataclan 2015-2016*. Paris, France: Anamosa.

Gensburger, S. (2018a). Beyond Trauma. Researching Memory on My Doorstep. In D. Drozdzewski & C. Birdsall (Eds.), *Doing Memory Research: New Methods and Approachs* (pp.109–128), Basingstoke, UK: Palgrave.

Gensburger, S. (2018b). Les archives comme matériaux commémoratifs. *La Gazette des Archives, 250*(2), 255–262.

Gensburger, S. (2020). Visiting History, Witnessing Memory. A study of a Holocaust Exhibition in Paris in 2012. *Memory Studies* (online first 2017).

Gensburger, S. (Ed.) (2013). Localiser le passé. *Genèses, 92*(3).

Gensburger, S., & Dybris McQuaid S. (2019). Administrations of memory: Transcending the nation and bringing back the state in memory studies. *Journal of Politics, Culture and Society, 2* (online first november 2019).

Gensburger, S., & Lefranc, S. (2017). À quoi servent les politiques de mémoire ? Paris, France: Presses de Sciences Po.

Ginzburg, C. (1989). *Mythes, emblèmes et traces. Morphologie et histoire.* Paris: Flammarion.

Goldberger, P. (2005). *Up from zero: politics, architecture, and the rebuilding of New York.* New York, NY: Random House.

Greene, V. (2011). *Cent vues de John Harvard.* Paris, France: L'attente.

Greene V., Uziel L. & Hollis, L. (2018). The Charlie Archive at Harvard Library: archiver de loin. *La Gazette des Archives, 250*(2), 63–82.

Halbwachs, M. ([1994], 1925). *Les cadres sociaux de la mémoire.* Paris, France: Albin Michel.

Halbwachs, M. (1938). *La Morphologie sociale.* Paris, France: Armand Colin.

Halbwachs, M. (1995). La mémoire collective chez les musiciens. In *La mémoire collective* (1st ed., 1950), Paris, France: Albin Michel.

Heath-Kelly, C (2016). *Death Security: Memory and Mortality at the Bombsite.* Manchester, UK: Manchester University Press.

Heath-Kelly, C. (2017). 'Resilience' and rituals bring people together, but our true reactions are more complex. *The Conversation.*

Hernandez, J. (2008). Le tourisme macabre à La Nouvelle-Orléans après Katrina: résilience et mémorialisation des espaces affectés par des catastrophes majeures. *Norois, 208*, 61–73.

Hetherington, K. (2007). Manchester's Urbis. *Cultural Studies, 21*(4-5), 630–649.

Hirsch, M. (2012). *The Generation of Postmemory: Writing and Visual Culture After the Holocaust.* New York, NY: Columbia University Press.

Hirst, W., & al. (2015). A Ten-year Follow-Up of a study of Memory for the Attack of September 11, 2001: Flashbulb Memories and Memories of Flashbulb Events. *Journal of Experimental Psychology: General, 144*(3), 604–623.

Hoibian, S., & al. (2018). L'emprunte des attentats du 13 novembre 2015 sur la société française. *Bull. Epidémiol Hebd, 38–39*, 772–781.

Huddy, L., & Feldman, S. (2011). Americans respond politically to 9/11: Understanding the impact of the terrorist attacks and their aftermath. *American Psychologist, 66*(6), 455–467.

Hughes, R. (2008). Dutiful tourism: Encountering Cambodian Genocide. *Asia Pacific Viewpoint, 49*(3), 318–330.

Huyssen, A. (2009). Memory Culture at an Impasse: Memorials in Berlin and New York. In W. Breckman & al. (Eds.), *The Modernist Imagination: Intellectual History and Critical Theory* (pp. 151–161). New York, NY: Berghahn Books.

Huyssen, A. (2003). *Present pasts: Urban palimpsests and the politics of memory* Stanford, CA: Stanford University Press.

Jackson, R., & Hall, G. (2016). Talking about terrorism: A study of vernacular discourse. *Politics, 36*(3), 292–307.

Jones, O., & Garde-Hansen, J. (Eds.) (2012). *Geography and Memory. Explorations in Identity, Place and Becoming.* Basingstoke, UK: Palgrave Macmillan.

Jouan, M. (2017). Politique du deuil: entre reconnaissance et invisibilisation. *Raison publique, 21*(1), 113–152.

Judaken, J. (2018). Judeophobia and Islamophobia in France Before and After Charlie Hebdo and Hyper Cacher. *Jewish History*, online first.

Kastoryano, R. (2005). *Les Codes de la différence, Race-Origine-Religion. France-Allemagne-États-Unis.* Paris, France: Presses de Sciences Po.

Klüger, R. (2010). *Le refus de témoigner.* Paris, France: Viviane Hamy.

La Révolution française, Cahier d'histoire de la Révolution française (2012). L'attentat objet d'histoire. *1.*

Lagadec, P., Le Gall, L., Simon, J. F., & Mannaig, T. (2019). Passage à l'acte: arborer un drapeau tricolore après les attentats du 13-Novembre (Brest, 27 novembre 2015). *Ethnologie Française.*

Lahire, B. (2016). *Pour la sociologie. Et pour en finir avec une prétendue « culture de l'excuse ».* Paris, France: La Découverte.

Laqueur T. (2016). *The Work of the Dead. A Cultural History of Mortal Remains.* Princeton: Princeton University Press.

Latté, S. (2012). La 'force de l'événement' est-elle un artefact ? Les mobilisations de victimes au prisme des théories événementielles de l'action collective. *Revue française de science politique, 62*(3), 409–432.

Lavabre, M. C. (1994). *Le Fil rouge. Sociologie de la mémoire communiste.* Paris, France: Presses de la Fondation nationale des sciences politiques.

Lavabre, M. C. (2000). Usages et mésusages de la notion de mémoire. *Critique internationale, 7*(1), 48–57.

Lefébure, P., & Sécail, C. (Eds.) (2016). *Le défi Charlie. Les médias à l'épreuve des attentats.* Paris, France: Lemieux éditeur.

Lefranc, S. (2013). Un tribunal des larmes. La Commission sud-africaine "Vérité et Réconciliation". October 8. Retrieved from http://www.laviedesidees.fr/Un-tribunal-des-larmes.html.

Lefranc, S., & Mathieu, L. (Eds.) (2009). *Mobilisations des victimes.* Rennes, France: Presses universitaires de Rennes.

Levitt, L. (2011). Speaking memory, building history: the influence of victims' families at the World Trade Center. *Radical History Review, 111,* 71–73.

Linenthal, E.T. (2001). *The Unifinished Bombing: Oklahoma City in American Memory.* New York, NY: Oxford University Press.

Lisle, D. (2004). Gazing at Ground Zero: Tourism, Voyeurism and Spectacle. *Journal for Cultural Research, 8*(1), 3–21.

Luminet, O., & Curci, A. (2017). *Flashbulb Memories: News Challenges and Future Perspectives.* Abingdon, UK: Routledge.

Macdonald, S. (2005). Accessing audiences: visiting visitor books. *Museum and society, 3*(3), 119–136.

Magry, P., & Sanchez-Carretero, C. (Eds.) (2011). *Grassroots Memorials: The Politics of Memorializing Traumatic Death.* Oxford, UK: Berghahn Books.

Maïlander, E. (2012). La violence des surveillantes des camps de concentration national-socialistes (1939–1945): réflexions sur les dynamiques et logiques du pouvoir. *Online Encyclopedia of Mass Violence.* Retrieved from http://www.massviolence.org/La-violence-des-surveillantes-des-camps-de-concentration.

Malandain, G. (2011). *L'introuvable complot. Attentat, enquête et rumeur dans la France de la Restauration.* Paris, France: Éditions de l'EHESS.

Margry, P. J., & Sánchez-Carretero, C. (2011). *Grassroots Memorials. The Politics of Memorializing Traumatic Death.* New York, NY: Berghahn Books.

Mazeau, G. (2009). *Le bain de l'histoire: Charlotte Corday et l'attentat contre Marat 1793-2009.* Paris, France: Champ Vallon.

Miles, W. F. S. (2002). Auschwitz: Museum Interpretation and Darker Tourism. *Annals of Tourism Research, 29*(4), 1175–1178.

Milosevic, A. (2017). Remembering the Present: Dealing with the Memory of Terroism in Europe. *Journal of Terrorism Research, 8*(4), 44–61.

Milosevic, A. (2018). Historicizing the present: Brussels attacks and heritagization of spontaneous memorials. *International Journal of Heritage Studies, 24*(1), 53–65.

Milstein, D. (2010). Children as co-researchers in anthropological narratives in education. *Ethnography and Education, 5*(1), 1–15.

Morin, S. A. (2015). *A Museum's Reference Guide to Collecting Spontaneous Memorials*. New England, Me: Museum Association.

Nevins, J. (2005). The Abuse of Memorialized Space and Redefinition of Ground Zero. *Journal of Human Rights, 4*(2), 267–282.

Nora, P. (Ed.) (1997). *Les lieux de mémoire*. Paris, France: Gallimard.

Oksanen A., Kaakinen M., Minkkinen J., Räsänen P., Enjolras B., & Steen-Johnsen K. (2018). Perceived Societal Fear and Cyberhate after the November 2015 Paris Terrorist Attacks. *Terrorism and Political Violence, 0*(0), 1-20.

Ortiz Garcia, C. (2013). Pictures that save, pictures that soothe: photographs at the grassroots memorials to the victims of the March 11, 2003 Madrid bombings. *Visual Anthropology Review, 29*(1), 57–71.

Osofsky, J., Kronenberg, M., Bochnek, E., & Cross Hansel, T. (2015). Longitudinal Impact at Attachment-Related Risk and Exposure to Trauma Among Young Children After Hurrican Katrina. *Child & Youth Care Forum, 44*(4), 493–510.

Perec, G. (2000). *Espèces d'espaces*. Paris, France: Galilée.

Perec, G. (2008). *Tentative d'épuisement d'un lieu parisien*. Paris, France: Bourgois.

Perego, S. (2016). Commemorating the Holocaust during the First Postwar Decade. Jewish Initiatives and non-Jewish Actors in France. In R. Fritz, E. Kovacs, & B. Rasky (Eds.), Before the Holocaust Had Its Name. Early Confrontations with the Nazi Mass Murder of the Jews / Als der Holocaust noch keinen Namen hatte. Zur frühen Aufarbeitung des NS-Massenmords an Jüdinnen und Juden (pp. 223–239), Vienne, Austria: New Academic Press.

Peschanski, D., & Eustache, F. (2016). "13-Novembre", un programme de recherché inédit sur les mémoires traumatiques. *Revue de neuropsychologie, 8*(3), 155–157.

Pink, S., Sumartojo, E., Lupton, D., Heyes LaBond (2017). Empathetic technologies: digital materiality and video ethnography. *Visual Studies, 32*, 371–381.

Pollak, M. (1993). *L'Experience concentrationnaire. Essai sur le maintien de l'identité sociale*. Paris: Métailié.

Reading, A. (2011). The London bombing: mobile witnessing, mortal bodies and globital time. *Memory Studies*, 4(3), 298–311.

Riley, A. (2014). Flags, Totem Bodies, and the Meanings of 9/11: A Durkheimian Tour of September 11th Ceremony at the Flight 93 Chapel. *Canadian Journal of Sociology*, *39*(4), 719–740.

Roubert, C. (2013). Les visiteurs photographes autour de la pierre de Rosette au British Museum. In S. Chaumier & al., *Visiteurs photographes au musée*, Paris, France: La Documentation française.

Rothberg M. (2009). *Multidirectional Memory. Remembering the Holocaust in the Age of Decolonization*. Stanford, CA: Stanford University Press.

Sagalyn, L. (2016). *Power at Ground Zero: politics, money, and the remaking of Lower Manhattan*. New York, NY: Oxford University Press.

Salomé, K. (2015). La France, scène du terrorisme international – 1982–2015. In E. Laurentin (ed.), *Comment en sommes-nous arrivés là ? Histoire d'une République fragile*. Paris, Fayard: 171–176.

Salomé, K. (2010). L'attentat de la rue Nicaise: l'émergence d'une violence iné-dite ? *La Revue d'histoire du XIXe siècle*, 40/1, 59–75.

Sánchez-Carretero, C. (2011). *El archivo del duelo: analisis de la respuesta ciu-dadana ante los atentados del 11 de marzo en Madrid*. Madrid, Spain: Consejo Superior de Investigaciones Cientificas.

Sánchez-Carretero, C., Cea, A., Díaz-Mas, P., Martínez, P., & Ortiz, C. (2011). On Blurred Borders and Interdisciplinary Research Teams: The Case of the 'Archive of Mourning'. *Qualitative Social Research*, *12*(3).

Santino, J. (2006). *Spontaneous shrines and the public memorialization of death*. New York, NY: Plagrave-Macmilan.

Santino, J. (2011). Between Commemoration and Social Activism: Spontaneous Shrines, Grassroots Memorialization, and the Public Ritualesque in Derry. In P. Magry & C. Sánchez-Carretero (Eds.), *Grassroots Memorials. The Politics of Memorializing Traumatic Death* (pp. 97–107), New York, NY: Berghahn Books.

Sardan de, J. P. O. (1995). La politique du terrain. *Enquête, 1*. Retrieved from http://enquete.revues.org

Senie, H. F. (2013). Commemorating the Oklahoma City Bombing: Reframing Tragedy as Triumph. *Public Art Dialogue*, *3*(1), 80–109.

Silken, A. (2007). The Impact of 9/11 on Research on Terrorism. In M. Ranstorp Mapping Terrorism Research: State of the Art, Gaps and Future Directions. New York, Abingdon: Routledge.

Siman-Tov, M., Bodas, M. & Peleg K. (2016) The Social Impact of Terrorism on Civilian Populations: Lessons Learned from Decades of Terrorism in Israel and Abroad. Social Science Quarterly, 97(1), 75–85.

Simko, C. (2015). The Politics of Consolation. Memory and the Meaning of September 11. Oxford, UK: Oxford University Press.

Simmel, G. (2004). Métropoles et mentalité. In Y. Grafmeyer & I. Joseph (Eds.), L'École de Chicago: naissance de l'écologie urbaine (1st ed. 1903, pp. 61–77). Paris, France: Flammarion.

Simpson, D. (2006). 9/11: the culture of commemoration. Chicago, Ill: University of Chicago Press.

Simpson, E., & Corbridge, S. (2006). The Geography of Things That May Become Memories: The 2001 Earthquake in Kachchh-Gujarat and the Politics of Rehabilitation in the Prememorial Era. Annals of the Association of American Geographers, 96(3), 566–585.

Smithsimon, G. (2011). September 12: Community and neighborhood at Ground Zero. New York, NY: New York University Press.

Sontag, S. (2003). Devant la douleur des autres. Paris, France: Christian Bourgois.

Sturken, M. (2007). Tourists of History: Memory, Kitsch, and Consumerism from Oklahoma City to Ground Zero. Durham NC: Duke University Press.

Sturken, M. (2015). The 9/11 Memorial Museum and the remaking of Ground Zero. American Quarterly, 67(2), 471–490.

Sturken, M. (2016). The objects that lived: The 9/11 Museum and material transformation. Memory Studies, 9(1), 13–26.

Talarico, J. M., & Rubin, D. C. (2017). Ordinary memory processes shape Flashbulb memories of extraordinary events: A review of 40 years of research. In O. Luminet, & A. Curci (Eds.), Flashbulb Memories: News Challenges and Future Perspectives, Abingdon: Routledge.

Taylor, D. (2003). The Archive and the Repertoire: Performing Cultural Memory in the Americas. Durham, NC: Duke University Press.

Tilly, C. (2004). Terror, Terrorism, Terrorists. Sociological Theory, 22(1), 5–13.

Tiryakian, E. A. (2005). Durkheim, solidarity, and September 11. In J.C. Aleksander & P. Smith (Eds.), The Cambridge companion to Durkheim, Cambridge, UK: Cambridge University Press, 305–321.

Tolia-Kelly, D., & Rose, G. (2012). Visuality/Materiality: Images, Objects and Practices. London, UK: Routledge.

Tornatore, J. L., & Barbe, N. (Eds.) (2011). *Les formats d'une cause patrimoniale. Agir pour le château de Lunéville.* Lahic/DPRPS-Direction générale des patrimoines.

Tota, A. L. (2004). Ethnographying Public Memory: The Commemorative Genre for the Victims of Terrorism in Italy. *Qualitative Research, 4*(2), 131–159.

Tota, A.L. (2003). *La città ferita. Memoria e commucazione pubblica della strage di Bologna, 2 agosto 1980*, Bologna, Il Mulino.

Tota, A.L. (2005). Terrorism and Collective Memories: comparing Bologna, Naples, Madrid 11 March. *International Journal of Comparative Sociology.* 46 (1–2), 55–78.

Truc, G. (2012). Memory of places and places of memory: for a Hwlbachsian socio-ethnography of collective memory. *International Social Science Journal, 203-204*, 147–159.

Truc, G. (2017a). Mémorialisations immédiates. *Mémoires en jeu, 4*, 47–49.

Truc, G. (2017b). Quel mémorial après un attentat de masse ? Trois capitales européennes faces au même défi mémorial. *Mémoires en jeu, 4*, 90–95.

Truc, G. (2018). *Shell Shocked. The Social Response to Terrorist Attacks.* Cambridge, UK: Polity Press.

Truc, G. (2019). Ce que les attentats font aux sociétés: enquêtes de terrain et études de cas. *Ethnologie française, XLIX*(1), 5–20.

Tulloch, J. (2006). *One Day in July: experiencing 7/7.* London, UK: Little Brown.

Urry, J (2002). *The Tourist Gaze.* London, UK: SAGE Publications.

Veyne, P. (2002). Lisibilité des images, propagande et apparat monarchique dans l'Empire romain. *Revue historique, 1*(621), 3–30.

Vidal-Ortiz, S. (2004). On Being a White Person of Color: Using Autoethnography to Understand Puerto Ricans' Racialization. *Qualitative Sociology, 27*(2), 179–203.

Wagner-Pacifici, R. (2010). Theorizing the Restlessness of Events. *American Journal of Sociology, 115*(5), 1351–1386.

Wagner-Pacifici, R., & Schwartz, B. (1991). The Vietnam Veterans Memorial: Commemorating a Difficult Past. *The American Journal of Sociology, 2*(97), 376–420.

Welzer, H. (2008). *Les Exécuteurs. Des hommes normaux aux meurtriers de masse.* Paris, France: Gallimard.

Woods, J. (2012). *Freaking out: a decade of living with terrorism.* Washington, DC: Potomac Books.

Yaeger, P. (2003). Rubble as archive, or 9/11 as dust, debris, and bodily bani-shing. In J. Greenberg (Ed.), *Trauma at Home: After 9/11*. New York: Bison Books.

Young, J. (2016). The memorial's arc: Between Berlin's Denkmal and New York City's 9/11 Memorial. *Memory Studies*, 9(3), 325–331.

Young, J.E. (2000) *At memory's edge: After-images of the Holocaust in contemporary art and architecture*. New Have, CT: Yale University Press.

Zamperini, A., & Passarella L. (2017). Testimony of terrorism: Civic responsibility and memory work after a political massacre. *Memory Studies*, on line first July 26.

Zerubavel, E. (2003). *Time Maps. Collective Memory and the Social Shape of the Past*. Chicago, IL: University of Chicago Press.

Zerubavel, Y. (1996). The Forest As a National Icon: Literature, Politics, and the Archeology of Memory. *Israel Studies*, 1(1), 60–99.

CPSIA information can be obtained
at www.ICGtesting.com
Printed in the USA
LVHW072004290419
615964LV00011B/152/P

9 789462 701342